# Mr Cardiff City:
# The Autobiography of
# Phil 'Joe' Dwyer

# Mr Cardiff City:
# The Autobiography of
# Phil 'Joe' Dwyer

Phil Dwyer
(with James Leighton)

Fort Publishing Ltd

First published in 2011 by Fort Publishing Ltd, Old Belmont House,
12 Robsland Avenue, Ayr, KA7 2RW

Graphics by Mark Blackadder

Typeset by Kerrypress Ltd

Printed by Ozgraf

ISBN: 978-1-905769-26-1

*For my beautiful wife, Ann*

# Contents

# Foreword

By
Len Ashurst

When I joined Cardiff City as manager in the early spring of 1982, I arrived at Ninian Park knowing that here was a unique opportunity for me to take charge of a great club. It would be an understatement to say I was disappointed by what I encountered during my first few weeks. The finances were perilous, the team was struggling, and, most importantly, the dressing room lacked discipline.

Phil Dwyer was one of the big names at the club, and I knew, from watching him play many times, that he was a very good centre half but by this stage he had lost his way. He had been playing through the pain barrier with a knee injury for some time and that had a detrimental effect on his form. I also felt that he hadn't bought into my way of thinking and that as he was a big character in the dressing room this could cause problems. Knowing that I had to completely overhaul the squad that summer I took the hard decision to release him.

Phil was obviously disappointed, but took the news well, and strived to continue his career at Torquay. Before long I was hearing reports that he was back to his best and that it was not too late to bring him home. I had certainly missed him as a player on the pitch, and as a character in the dressing room, and therefore I made a move to re-sign him. He returned to Cardiff City duly humbled from his experience and with a determined new attitude. Having put him in the team at Walsall he proceeded to score one of the goals in a 2–1 victory. He and I never looked back.

I brought some very successful new signings into the club that summer, such as Jeff Hemmerman, Roger Gibbins and Paul Bodin, but perhaps Phil turned out to be my most important addition. That season Phil hit the best form of his career as Cardiff City were promoted after only one season in the old third division. However, it wasn't his level of play that impressed me the most but the fact that he finally became the leader which had been simmering in him for so long.

On the pitch Phil was a Trojan, driving his teammates on, battling for an elusive winner or demanding that bit extra to enhance a win. I will always remember the game we played against Newport County that season, which we won 3–2, on a mud heap of a pitch. We were holding on to a slender lead and time after time Phil Dwyer flung himself on to the muddy surface in defending his goal, as wave after wave of attacks were repelled by his bravery and unselfishness. This was the reason why every manager who handled him accepted his little idiosyncrasies as they knew they were getting more than they could ask for when he pulled on the blue jersey.

Off the pitch he was also the life and soul of the club. The late Harry Parsons, our humorous, beloved kit man, would frequently be at the end of Phil's wind-ups, and he would bustle out of the changing room, with a few choice expletives, but would always take the banter in the nature it was intended, a bit of fun. Phil was at home whenever there was humour and a laugh to be had and he kept the dressing-room atmosphere on the 'bubble'.

To sum up my opinion of the man, when I departed, to take up the managerial role at my former club, first division Sunderland, if Phil had been younger he would have been the first player I would have signed. As it was, it turned out that my target was to be Gary Bennett!

Phil, I wish you well with your autobiography, don't be too hard on me when you relate the story of your release. I know your wife was sore at the time, as she confronted me in the director's box at Ninian Park, and had the bottle to poke her finger into my chest in front of the home supporters, and demand that I put you back in the team where you belonged. She had more than a few people agreeing with her as well!

Good luck and good health.

**Len Ashurst**

** Len Ashurst's acclaimed autobiography, *Left Back in Time*, which he wrote himself to coincide with his seventieth birthday, was published in 2009 and is available to buy on Amazon and from www.lenashurst.com

# Acknowledgements

First and foremost I have to thank my fabulous parents, Ted and Connie, who taught me right from wrong and instilled in me a sense of discipline, graft and fun. My wonderful sister, Maureen, and her late husband, Derrick, also played a huge part in my upbringing and were always there for me. Without their help I doubt I would have played one game for Cardiff City, let alone hundreds.

Ann, my patient and understanding wife, and our two beautiful children, Darren and Claire, have also stuck by me through thick and thin. They have provided me with some of my happiest times and to this day I love them all dearly, who knows where I would be without them. My two little grandchildren, Luca and Erin, have also brought plenty of joy to my life and I'm looking forward to seeing them grow up. I must also thank Ann's late parents, Frank and Pat, both mad Cardiff City fans, who were the best parents-in-law anyone could have asked for as they treated me like a son and really made me feel part of the family.

As for those who helped me in my football career the list really could be endless, but I must acknowledge the help of Harry Parsons and Jimmy Scoular, who spotted me, trained me and then gave me my chance. Both are Cardiff City legends, and in my eyes they deserve every plaudit that they receive. Gary Bell, my old Cardiff City pal, has also been a great friend over the years and has provided me with plenty of support and laughter.

Finally, I must thank you, the Cardiff City fans, who always stuck by me, and made me feel the luckiest man in the world. Being able to pull on that famous blue shirt every week, and play in front of you, was a real thrill. I can't tell you how much it meant to me.

It is impossible to list everyone who has helped me keep my chin up over the years, but I would still like to thank you all from the bottom of my heart for believing in me. I couldn't have done it without you.

Phil Dwyer
Cardiff
June 2011

# Introduction

For thirteen years I wore the blue shirt of Cardiff City with immense pride. I was just a working class, Grangetown boy, who happened to be decent at football, and wanted more than anything in the world to play for my hometown club. Thankfully, my dream came true. Hundreds of times I strode out onto the Ninian Park pitch, to the roar of a full house, chanting my name, conscious of the fact that I wasn't just living out my dream, but also that of all Cardiff fans.

To this day I still can't quite believe that I ended up playing more times for Cardiff City than anyone else. It's incredible. If you had told me that, when I was fourteen, and struggling to get into the Cardiff Schools team, or when I was a schoolboy, under Jimmy Scoular, and on the verge of being released, I would never have believed you. I used to watch the likes of Don Murray, Gary Bell and Bobby Woodruff in awe and then all of a sudden they were my mates and I was playing alongside them.

Throughout my time as a Bluebird I must have seen just about everything. I've stood on the Bob Bank as a fan, watching us play against the best teams in Europe, and then experienced countless relegations and promotions as a player. It was a rollercoaster of emotions; at times I felt like tearing my hair out, while at others I wanted to drink every bar in St Mary Street dry. However, when something good did happen it was worth all the pain I had gone through, especially when I saw the joy it gave to the fans.

My relationship with the supporters has always been something I have treasured. Ever since I made my debut against Leyton Orient, in 1972, they took me into their hearts, and made me feel special. I hope that over the course of my career I have repaid their faith in me.

Talking in this book about some of the chants and banter, and the crazy things I've been asked to sign by supporters, has really made me laugh and emphasised just how fortunate Cardiff City Football Club are to have the best fans in the country.

Writing this book has also allowed me to reminisce, not only about matches and incidents that all Cardiff fans remember, but also to reveal stories that have never been told. I like to think that I have laid bare my time at Ninian Park: from punch ups in the changing room, rows with managers, pranks among the players, almost dying on the pitch and even a potential move to Greek giants, Panathinaikos.

Of course I was also lucky enough to be called upon to represent my country, playing against greats such as Kenny Dalglish and Kevin Keegan. Turning out for Wales also meant that I shared a dressing room with Swansea's Alan Curtis and Leighton James, which made life really interesting, particularly when international duty was over, as I used to take great pleasure in kicking a moaning Leighton up in the air in South Wales derby games. As I will reveal, it was not the games against Swansea that gave me any bother, rather it was the clashes with Newport County, in which a young striker by the name of John Aldridge provoked me to commit an assault on a football pitch.

Dealing with assaults became a full-time job because after I retired from football I joined the South Wales police, which was frequently hair-raising. Used to the adulation of the crowd it was a bit different dealing with criminals, who wanted to do me harm, but, after playing against the likes of Joe Jordan, I knew how to take care of myself.

Anyway, all of that is to come. I sincerely hope you enjoy reading about my time at Cardiff City and I'd like to thank you all for your unbelievable support over the years.

# 1

# Grangetown Boy

Ironically, I entered the world doing something that I would later make a living from: kicking and screaming. The date was 28 October 1953 and I was born in the family flat, in Grangetown, Cardiff. At the time, Cardiff City – the club that I would one day make a record number of appearances for – were one of the top sides in the country. During the year of my birth they caused a stir by signing Wales international, Trevor Ford, from Sunderland, for a British record fee of £30,000, and also beat Liverpool, 1–0, at Anfield, to relegate them from the first division. It was a great time to be a City supporter.

However, the city of Cardiff itself was not enjoying such a great time. Following the Second World War, South Wales suffered from a harsh recession, due to the demand for coal plummeting, which caused the once thriving docks to grind to a standstill. As a result, with little work around, many struggled and the working-class area where I was born, Grangetown, suffered more than most.

Despite these hard times Grangetown was a great place to live. Before the recession people had come from all over the world to work in the docks and many had settled in the area. With so many cultures it was often an eye opener, but I can never recall there being any bother. Everyone seemed to know everyone else and just mucked in. There was a real community spirit and if you were ever in trouble, or needed something, you were never short of a friend.

Grangetown may have been a tough area, but crime was nowhere near the level it is today. We could leave our doors unlocked because burglaries were virtually unheard of. Most families would leave their house key dangling from a piece of string, just behind the letterbox, so that if the door was locked all you needed to do was stick your hand through the slot and grab it. Your house wouldn't stand a chance if you were to do that today.

My family's flat was situated on Penarth Road, between Teddy Young's fruit store on one corner and the Grange pub on the other. Our tiny living quarters consisted of a basement, where we had our kitchen, the ground floor, which was our living room, and then a second floor, where we all slept. It was basic, but it was home.

As you have probably noticed I haven't mentioned a bathroom, simply because there wasn't one. If we needed a wash we would have to go to the basement/kitchen and fill an old tin bath with hot water, which we had boiled on the stove. The thought of having a bath in the middle of a kitchen seems bizarre now, but in those days it wasn't that unusual. Filling the bath would, however, take forever and as I was so impatient I usually made do with a wet flannel.

Saving time wasn't the only reason to avoid the dreaded bath. In my youth not many of the houses in Grangetown had central heating and our house was no different. Washing in the hot bath water would briefly get me warm, but getting out afterwards would be hell. I would stand there, covered in towels, shivering like a drowned rat.

Thankfully, we had a coal fire in our living room, so in the winter we would all crowd around it. If we ran out of coal I would be sent outside to get a sack of the black stuff from our coal hole, which was situated under a manhole cover at the front of the house. Unfortunately, with no central heating, or double glazing, the winter nights could be very harsh. I remember that sometimes there used to be ice on the inside of the windows and even with six blankets over me my teeth would still be chattering.

Living in the house at the time were my mum, dad and my sister, Maureen. I also had three brothers, Kenny, Peter and Brian, but they were quite a bit older than me and had moved out by the time I was born. This was actually a bonus as it meant that I got my own bedroom, which was a real treat, as most of my mates would be crammed into rooms with their brothers or sisters.

In spite of my three older brothers not living with us I got on well with all of them. As in most families there is always a black sheep and I suppose Kenny was ours. He always seemed to be getting himself into trouble, nothing too serious, but at times he caused my parents no end of grief. In my eyes he was as good as gold but I suppose you love your brother no matter what. I always enjoyed it when he came over as he would make a real fuss of me but, unfortunately, Kenny died at a young age due to diabetes, which was a real blow.

I didn't really see too much of Peter when I was a kid, as he joined the armed forces, and spent a lot of time away. However, whenever he did come home, I loved to listen to him talk about his adventures fighting for his country. Even as a young kid I respected him so much; we all did.

Out of all of my brothers I was probably closest to Brian when I was growing up. Before I came along he was the real sportsman in the family. He was one of the star players for St Patrick's FC, when they were probably the top amateur side in Cardiff, and arguably the best football team outside of the Welsh League. Thanks to their prowess St Pat's always got decent crowds and I would go along to cheer him on. Brian was always very quick and had an eye for a goal. I thought he was a superstar.

While Brian was an excellent amateur footballer, his real talent lay in boxing. He was so good that he turned professional and even boxed for Wales at the Empire Games, which made all of Grangetown proud. As I used to look up to Brian I also tried my hand at boxing, but I soon packed it in when I realised that I didn't like getting hit! To this day Brian is still involved with the Welsh Boxing Board, where over the years he has done a tremendous job.

As my brothers had moved out, I spent a lot of time with my sister, and I like to think that we developed a very close relationship. I'm not sure, however, if she remembers my early years so fondly. Like my brothers, Maureen was quite a bit older than me, and she was at an age when she would rather be hitting the town than looking after a baby brother. When I was still a toddler she was a good looking teenager, with no shortage of offers from young men to take her out. With Mum and Dad being at work it meant that she couldn't leave me by myself so I would sometimes have to tag along with her on her dates, which inevitably cramped her style. Sometimes I think Dad must have done it on purpose because with me accompanying her no one could take advantage. It was a smart move. While I no doubt got on her nerves we spent a lot of time together and that has meant we are still very close to this day.

I was lucky that I was also very close to Mum and Dad, although I had a very different relationship with the two of them, as they were such contrasting characters. They met in Tonypandy, when Mum was just a teenager, and Dad was a few years older. Shortly after meeting they got married and started a family. Dad found it hard to make ends meet, as he worked as a miner, which was backbreaking work for a low wage, so he decided to move the family to the bright lights of Cardiff. Eventually he found work at the foundry, in Tremorfa, which was still hard shift work, but the money and conditions were certainly better than working down the mines. Mum also started to work in a canteen, for a company that manufactured aluminium, and she was very popular there.

You may have thought that it would be quiet in the house without my three brothers, but you would be wrong. Mum, whose name was Constance, but whom everyone called Connie, was a real livewire. Like me, she could never sit still; she was constantly on the go and always chatting away.

Nearly all of her energy went on looking after other people, she never thought of herself. If we had visitors she would insist on making them something, if they refused she almost saw it as an insult. When she wasn't spending her time cooking in the kitchen, or cleaning up after us, she would knit clothes. Sat in our small living room, listening to *The Archers* on the radio, she would spend hours furiously knitting away. Some of her efforts were actually very nice, but others were horrendous, Christmas-style jumpers that led to me getting slaughtered by my mates.

Music was always big in our house and my mum loved it. If she wasn't talking she would be singing and dancing to the music on the radio. If we went out she would always be the first up on the dance floor, and, to my intense embarrassment, she would usually drag me up there with her. Dancing has never been one of my strong points; I'm like a slug getting electrocuted by a cattle prod! Mum loved music so much that she also played the tambourine in the Salvation Army band and encouraged me to learn an instrument.

When I started going to St Patrick's primary school I joined the band in an effort to please her, and partly because I fancied myself as a drummer. Mum was delighted and she scrimped and saved to buy me a brand-new set of drumsticks. Within seconds of receiving them I was so excited I took them out with me and started banging them against the wall. In the middle of a drum solo I banged one of them a little too hard and the tip fell off. I tried my best to hide it but, as always, Mum eventually found out, and I received a rollicking for being so careless.

If Mum needed time to relax from keeping me in line she would head off with her friends to the Dominion bingo hall, which was just across the road. She rarely won but I think she enjoyed the social side of it more than anything. I swear I could hear her laugh even when I was sat in my bedroom.

Her big personality wasn't, however, matched by her size as she was very petite. She was a beautiful woman, who looked timid on the surface, but she ruled the house with a rod of iron. If you got on the wrong side of her, God help you. I suppose she went a little easier on me because I was the youngest but there was never any chance of me stepping out of line, because even if I managed to butter her up, I would still have Dad to answer to.

Dad was completely different to Mum. He was a massive bloke, built like a brick shit house, and more than six-feet-six-inches tall. When I was young I was terrified of him, particularly if I disturbed him when he was trying to sleep after working a nightshift. While Mum would always be talking, Dad was far more reserved and kept to himself. Despite this we got on very well as we enjoyed the same things. One of my earliest memories is helping him out with his pigeons, which he kept in a loft in our back garden. It would always amaze me that we could let the pigeons fly away, and they could go all over the place, yet they would always return.

Our mutual love for sport was, however, the thing that really brought Dad and me together. We were both crazy for it. Every Saturday we would spend hours watching *Grandstand* in our living room. His big treat for the week was having a bet on the horses and then watching the race on television. In the morning he would methodically scour the *Racing Post* before giving me some coins, so that I could run off to the local bookies and put a bet on for him. He would be at his most animated when the racing came on. I can see him now, sat in his favourite armchair, in front of the telly, with his pipe in his mouth, and the *Racing Post* in his hand, shouting excitedly. As the race neared the end he would jump up and down, urging his horse on. He rarely won, and if he did it wouldn't be much, but he loved the excitement.

Another sport that gave us great pleasure was wrestling, which would usually follow the horse racing. Our favourite wrestlers were Jackie 'Mr Television' Pallo, Billy Two Rivers and Mick McManus. While Dad cheered for Mick McManus, because he was as hard as nails, my idol was a wrestler called Les Kellett. Les would always pretend that he was on the verge of being knocked out, and he would stagger around the ring, enticing the other wrestler towards him in order to finish him off. When his opponent got close enough Les would make a miraculous recovery and proceed to pin him down to secure an improbable win. Looking back I can see just how ridiculous it was but it was great entertainment and it never failed to get Dad and me out of our seats shouting at the television.

My parents didn't earn a lot of money so foreign holidays, eating out at restaurants and extravagant gifts were out of the question, but I never felt hard done by. There was always food on the table, clothes on our backs and most importantly a loving atmosphere. Compared to many I was living a life of luxury. With money being tight I always looked forward to the summer holidays as it gave me a rare opportunity to get out of Cardiff. Just getting away for the day was a huge adventure. I would be so excited you would have thought I was going on a luxury cruise. As Mum and Dad still had plenty of friends and family living in Tonypandy we spent a lot of time there. I suppose it was a mark of how popular Mum and Dad were that they were always warmly greeted on their return. Everyone used to meet at a place called the Rioja Club and I would just sit there quietly, with a bottle of pop and a packet of crisps, and people would remark how much I looked like my mum, who, like I say, was a good-looking lady!

Going on day trips to places like Lavernock and Barry Island were also huge treats. To me those places were on the other side of the world. More often than not the whole street would go together, which was great, as I would have all my mates from Grangetown with me. Namely, Michael Rain, Phillip O'Hara, Brian Milford, Glyn Jones and Charlie Deakins, who we nicknamed 'Jelly Bean' because he was really tall, but wouldn't hurt a fly.

As a youngster I used to love visiting Glyn's house. His dad, Taffy, was a rag-and-bone man who would go around the neighbourhood on his horse and cart, selling second-hand goods. When I went to Glyn's house I could never wait to rummage through all the random things his dad was trying to sell. You used to find all sorts in there.

Barry Island was probably my favourite destination when we went on a day out as not only would we all have a big game of football on the beach, while the parents had a drink and a smoke, but we would also visit the fun fair. We didn't have much money for the rides so we used to sneak on as many of them as possible. One attraction that never failed to amaze me was a motorbike stunt show called The Wall of Death. The rider would be zooming around a circular wall, on his bike, at all sorts of angles and I could never understand how he managed to keep his balance. I would stand there for ages marvelling at his prowess.

Another excursion we all enjoyed, but couldn't really afford, was our weekly trip to the Ninian cinema, which was just down the road. All week I would be champing at the bit for Saturday morning to come, particularly if there was a science-fiction film on the double bill. It was not unusual for us be in the cinema for five hours at a time but I was so engrossed it flew by. After watching a film we were so wound up that we would head up to the woods, at the top of Penarth Road, where we would act out our favourite scenes. Depending on what we had just seen the woodland would be transformed into a desert island, a jungle or even the Wild West. I remember building forts and tree houses, and having pretend wars, which sometimes could get out of hand, particularly if I was feeling extra boisterous.

Some weeks we couldn't afford the cinema entry fee, or had spent our money on sweets, so we would need to devise an alternative way in. Our usual plan would see us cobble together some coins, which would then allow one of the boys to pay the entry fee. Once that person was inside the theatre they would sneak behind the screen curtain and open the exit doors so that we could all pile in. Occasionally, we would get caught by the irate manager, and would have to leg it, but the rewards were well worth the risk. If our mission was successful we would gorge ourselves on sweets and ice cream, which would be carried by an usherette on a tray.

If we couldn't afford sweets then we made do with the 'free' food that Grangetown had to offer. Back then a lot of people still grew vegetables and fruit in their gardens and allotments, allowing us to help ourselves. A favourite pastime was to pinch the apples that would be hanging from trees over garden walls. One of the boys would give another one a bunk up and they would grab the apples and throw them down. Getting spotted was an occupational hazard but we were all so quick that the owners could never catch us.

The fact that we had such little money meant that sometimes we would get into trouble. We weren't bad kids, but if we could get something for nothing then we would. Despite getting away with most of our 'crimes' there was one occasion on which I wasn't so lucky, when I was caught shoplifting in town. I can't even remember what I tried to pinch, but the police got hold of me and took me home, which was in my eyes a worse punishment then being sent away. I was sure that Mum and Dad would go crazy and I was proved right. The moment the police left the house I tried to leg it to my room but Dad got hold of me and smacked me with his belt. After that my shoplifting days were officially over.

It wasn't just Dad who administered punishment of that sort if I misbehaved; my teachers could also dish it out. I wasn't a bad kid, but I couldn't sit still in lessons and was easily distracted. I have lost count of the number of times I would be chatting away when all of a sudden I would be hit by a piece of chalk or a duster. If one of those flying objects hit me on the head, which it did from time to time, it would bring tears to my eyes. Sometimes a chalk duster to the head wasn't a severe enough punishment so I would be sent to the headmaster, who would cane me across the backside. I received that punishment a number of times and, believe me, it stung.

Looking back, it seems draconian, but I can honestly say it didn't do me any harm. If anything it served to keep me on the straight and narrow. We had genuine respect for our parents, elders, police and teachers, which I don't think you get today. If we stepped out of line we knew we would get punished and that served as a real deterrent. These days some of the punishments are a joke.

Having so much energy meant that I was always looking for something to do, and because of this, sport became a huge part of my life. I would play cricket, baseball, rugby and tennis for hours in the street or if it was too cold the boys and I would go down to the North Clive Street youth club for a game of table tennis or to the local snooker hall for a few frames. Football was, however, beyond a shadow of a doubt my favourite sport. Nearly every spare minute I had was taken up by the game. For hours on end my mates and I would play in the street, with no one keeping score. Winning or losing didn't matter; we played because we loved it. As leather balls were so expensive we had to use whatever we could get our hands on, which would usually turn out to be a tennis ball. However, using such a small ball, on an uneven surface, certainly improved my technique.

If we got lucky, and had a leather ball to play with, we would use it until it was scuffed down to the bladder. These days everyone seems to be complaining about how light the ball is, but I would like to see the players of today cope with the old balls. On a wet day the ball would soak up the water so it would become too heavy to kick very far. You would certainly struggle to see the likes of David Beckham hitting seventy-yard cross-field passes with it. The worst thing about the leather balls was heading them. Not only would they make your ears ring, and give you a headache, but also if you headed the lace you would have the imprint on your forehead for days afterwards.

My parents could see that I was obsessed with the game so Mum saved up the money to buy me a pair of football boots. I think she got them from a shop in Cardiff central market. They weren't anything special, just plain black leather, but I felt like a proper player in them. Walking onto a field in those boots made me feel ten feet tall and my mates were all jealous.

Growing up I didn't think that I was better than anyone else. However, looking back, it was obvious that I had a talent. Every Sunday morning the older lads would organise an eleven-a-side game at Sevenoaks Park, where the boys from Lower Grangetown would take on their peers from Upper Grangetown. The rivalry was always fierce and there were some very good players involved, but despite being a lot younger than everyone else I was always invited to play. Those games certainly toughened me up because no one cared if I was the youngest on the pitch. They still clattered me.

As a kid I didn't care about the position I played, as long as I was on the pitch. However, wherever I was picked, I seemed to do well. I was big for my age, and some people may laugh at this, but I was also very quick. In fact I always did well running the 100 and 200 metres on school sports day, although any further than that and I wasn't interested. With my size and pace I had the perfect attributes to play in either defence or attack. Back then I would play for both my primary-school team and North Clive youth club on the same day. I would usually play one game up front for one team and then at centre back for the other team. I used to do pretty well as a forward, and scored a few goals, but as the years passed it soon became clear that my best position was at the back.

Playing the game wasn't enough. Whenever I saw a match on telly, or read an article in a football magazine, I would be transfixed. Television coverage of the game in those days was unfortunately nowhere near modern standards. In fact, *Match of the Day* only started in 1964, and even then it would just be the highlights from one match. Thankfully, the FA Cup final would be shown in full every year and I would lap up every last minute. Coverage began at eleven in the morning and I would be sat in front of the telly all day, not moving an inch.

Finals in those days were gripping affairs, with the FA Cup the trophy everyone wanted to win. I don't think I can remember the last good final that I watched – as these days it's all about the Champions League – but back then it was the be all and end all. Two finals from my childhood that have always stayed in my mind are West Ham United versus Preston North End in 1964 and Sheffield Wednesday versus Everton in 1966. Both were dramatic games that had me leaping around the living room.

West Ham were the hot favourites in 1964 but they had to come from behind twice before finally scoring a late winner to defeat Preston of the second division. The 1966 final also saw Everton perform a thrilling comeback as they overcame a two-goal deficit and then went on to win the game, thanks to a late goal from Derek Temple. One of my future Cardiff City colleagues, Brian Harris, actually played in that final, which he never tired of reminding everyone. In fact he was so proud of it that he wore his cup-final medal around his neck until the day he died!

The one football event that received plenty of television coverage, and had the whole country hooked, was of course the 1966 World Cup. Despite Wales not being involved most people in Cardiff wanted England to do well, and I was no different. I have always supported the home nations in any tournament that we are not involved in and have never understood those who choose not to. After all, we're all British.

That World Cup was an unbelievable experience. Whenever there was a game on television the country would come to a standstill. Portugal, Brazil and England were the glamour teams, but I really enjoyed watching the plucky North Koreans. Although no one had ever heard of them they beat Italy in the group stages, and then lost a thrilling quarter final to Portugal, 5–3, after being 3–0 up. England, with the likes of Bobby Moore, Geoff Hurst and Bobby Charlton, won the tournament, beating West Germany 4–2, in a tremendously exciting final. After the game I was so overjoyed that I ran outside to join in an impromptu street game. Everyone was on such a high you would have thought that Wales, and not England, had become world champions.

Watching those FA Cup finals, and the World Cup, had me dreaming of one day playing at Wembley. Everything about it inspired me. The iconic twin towers, the national anthem, the perfect pitch (far removed from the usual mud heaps we played on), the fanatical supporters and then climbing those famous Wembley steps to lift a trophy. It summed up what the beautiful game was all about.

My football dreams were further fuelled by the tales of Roy Race in my favourite comic, *Roy of the Rovers*. I would spend hours on my doorstep, transfixed by his incredible feats on the football pitch. One day, I thought, I will be just like Roy Race, scoring wonder goals for my team in cup finals.

Watching televised games, and reading football magazines, provided me with my first real hero: Billy Bremner. Billy was the inspirational captain of Leeds United, one of the country's top sides, and when I was growing up I idolised him. Whenever I played I tried to copy his combative persona and I like to think that his burning will to win rubbed off on me. My small bedroom was covered, not only in posters of Billy, but also of the rest of that fantastic Leeds team of the late 1960s and early 1970s. In my eyes they were gods.

Another footballer that I and every other football fan in the country admired was George Best. The things that guy could do with a ball astounded me. It seemed as if the ball was tied to his boots with a piece of string. Later in my career I was lucky enough to be on the same pitch as George when he was winding down his career at Fulham. Although we beat Fulham 2–1, at Craven Cottage, it was clear that Bestie was still a top player. Although some help from yours truly may have helped him out. We were cruising and had a 2–0 lead, when, with five minutes to go, I picked up the ball on the halfway line and tried to play a back pass to our keeper. Disastrously, it went straight to the last person you would want it to go to, George Best. He raced clear and nonchalantly passed the ball into the net to make the score 2–1. We managed to hang on for the win but those last couple of minutes went by very slowly. After the game the lads slaughtered me. George didn't need a helping hand from anyone; he was a match winner on his own.

While I loved playing and watching the game on television I soon found that there was no substitute for a live match at Ninian Park. From a very early age my mates and I would go to watch as many Cardiff City games as we could, although unsurprisingly we rarely paid to get in. Over the years we developed countless ploys. Our favourite ruse would see us go around the back of the bus station on Sloper Road, get hold of a railway sleeper, put it up against a wall and then clamber over onto the Bob Bank. However, if there were no railway sleepers available, or if someone was watching, then we would have to try and sneak onto the Grange End.

In those days the Grange End stretched all the way to the houses at the back of the stand. Between the stand and the houses was a gap no bigger than a few yards but as we were so small we could fit in. One by one we would squeeze down the gap, armed with a 'borrowed' ladder, so that we could scale the twelve-foot Grange End wall. If a ladder wasn't readily available we would club together and raise a few pennies in order to persuade one of the house owners near the ground to lend us one.

In these days of all-seater stadiums it is hard to imagine that fans used to stand on terraces. Watching a game wasn't always the most comfortable experience, especially if you were small, because you would be crammed up against adults, which restricted the view. But it certainly made for a tremendous atmosphere. I remember one game in the Cup, in the early 1960s, when Cardiff drew Arsenal at Ninian Park, and the ground was jam packed. After the game, when the crowd was moving towards the exits, I was squashed so tight that I was literally lifted off my feet and carried out of the stadium. If I had fallen there would have been no saving me.

Although Cardiff had been relegated from the top flight in 1962 there were still plenty of good times to be had. Stars such as Ivor Allchurch, Peter Hooper and Derek Tapscott still graced the club and we had usually had European football to look forward to, thanks to our consistency in the Welsh Cup. In consequence, we were treated to some of the best teams from the Continent at Ninian Park. Crack sides such as Sporting Lisbon and Real Zaragoza came to town and had the fans clamouring to watch. The matches were always tight affairs but at home Cardiff actually managed to beat Lisbon, and drew with Zaragoza.

However, the game that will forever stay fixed in my mind came in 1968, when we reached the semi-final of the European Cup Winners Cup. Standing in the way of Cardiff City reaching their first European final was SV Hamburg, who had the great West Germany international, Uwe Seeler, in their ranks. Having drawn 1–1 in Hamburg there was confidence that we could win the game at Ninian Park and go onto the final. The excitement leading up to the match reached fever pitch and the atmosphere at the ground was electric.

As ever, when the stakes are high, Cardiff City always somehow manage to disappoint and that night was no different. With ten minutes remaining City were 2–1 down, but Brian Harris equalised, and we looked to have the momentum to finish them off. However, there was a nasty sting in the tail, because, in the final minute, Honig let fly from all of thirty yards. The shot was fired straight at our keeper, Bob

Wilson, and I remember it was so innocuous that I looked away. I fully expected Bob to gather it into his body, as he was a very accomplished keeper, and then launch the ball up the field for a final attack. But the ball squirmed from his grasp and spun into an empty net at the Canton Stand end. I felt numb. A deathly silence hung over the massive crowd, who had been tearing the roof off a few moments earlier. After all the build up I left Ninian Park that night in a state of total dejection.

No matter how distraught I was at a result I would always be back for the next game. Football was a drug. The whole experience intoxicated me. With the likes of Brian Harris, Don Murray, Greg Farrell, John Charles, Peter King and John Toshack lighting up Ninian Park it was hard to stay away. I loved Don Murray; he encapsulated everything I wanted to be on a football pitch. Everyone who has followed the club will remember him fondly; he led by example and in the eyes of Cardiff fans could do no wrong. I loved watching him fly into tackles, intimidating the opposition in the process. He was my inspiration.

Winger Greg Farrell was an entirely different player to Don, but he was also one of my favourites. He was a real livewire, and while in some games he could be anonymous, in others he would be out of this world. One game in which he was really on song was when Cardiff beat Middlesbrough 5–3 in 1966. He was untouchable. In one of the greatest performances I have ever seen he set up four goals and scored the other. The Middlesbrough players couldn't get near him, not even to kick him.

Perhaps the greatest player I saw play at Cardiff City, and I'm sure there won't be too many arguments, was the 'Gentle Giant', the great John Charles, who on his debut scored from all of seventy-five yards. The man was so big he made my dad look small. With thighs like oak trees and a huge barrel chest, he strode around the pitch like a colossus. But he also had wonderful technique, and could read the game like no one else. I once met him outside Ninian Park and I recall that as I shook his hand it was so massive that it completely engulfed mine. His nickname was certainly appropriate because despite having such a formidable physique he always had time to speak to the fans and was a real gentleman to everyone who came across him.

Watching all of these great players, and the exhilarating games, had me dreaming of one day playing on that Ninian Park pitch. It seemed like an outlandish dream, because despite being one of the better players for my age no team seemed to be interested in me. In fact, it wasn't until my teenage years, at Bishop Mostyn high school, that I really began to stand out. It started me on a path that would lead me from playing on the streets of Grangetown to playing in front of the Grange End.

# 2

# The Breakthrough

While I excelled at sport at Bishop Mostyn high school, I didn't distinguish myself academically. It wasn't that I was incapable in the classroom, because I don't think I was in the bottom sets for any subjects. It's just that I wasn't interested. I did enough to get by and nothing more. The only subject I enjoyed was science, as I got to play with chemicals and bunsen burners, although that did earn me a few trips to the headmaster's office.

Despite my less than sterling academic reputation, it didn't prevent my PE teacher, Mr Evans, from putting me into most of the school sports teams. For a time I played quite a bit of rugby and Mr Evans used to get the likes of Gerald Davies, who would go on to become a legend for Wales, to coach the team. As in football, I played a variety of positions on the rugby field: from full back to centre to winger. In one game I was even picked to play second row but I didn't have a clue what I was doing. I would try to push the scrum forwards, with my back to it, as if I was pushing a car!

During my teenage years I was constantly involved in sport. Midweek I would play rugby and on Saturdays I would play football for the school in the morning and then for North Clive Street youth club in the afternoon. Playing two games in one day never bothered me; I would have played three if it was possible. Baseball was also a sport I loved and in the summer I turned out for the local team, Grange Catholics, as well as representing Cardiff. At one stage I even thought that I was in with a shot of playing for Wales, but unfortunately I hurt my ankle and missed my chance. Most of my teams turned out to be quite successful and I managed to win a number of trophies.

On the odd occasion, when I wasn't playing sport, you would find me and the lads down the snooker club, at the youth club or hanging out at the Black and White café in Grangetown. As we got a bit older we would occasionally try our luck at getting some booze at the Baroness pub, just off Penarth Road, but we rarely succeeded, probably due to the horrendous bum-fluff moustaches that we had spent weeks growing and our feeble attempt at putting on deep, manly voices.

Getting booze was usually out of the question so, as an alternative, a night the lads and me always looked forward to would be the underage disco in the Top Rank nightclub on Queen Street. We would get ourselves into our best gear – usually drainpipe jeans, winkle-picker shoes and Ben Sherman shirt – and chat up anything that moved. I was hardly Don Juan. In fact, my best line was, 'So, do you come here often?' as I tried to look cool leaning against the bar.

With lines like that it is amazing it was actually at Top Rank that I met my first girlfriend, who would also turn out to be my future wife. On the 'luckiest' night of her life I was at the bar with my two friends, Jimmy Hobby and Kevin Cruise, when I spotted this gorgeous, petite brunette. As luck would have it she was friends with Kevin's sister, Linda, so she came over to say hello. We started chatting and I found out that her name was Ann. While initially nothing happened between us we kept bumping into each other and eventually we started dating. As the weeks went by we became inseparable and our relationship got serious. For the first time in my life there was something that rivalled my love for sport and I found myself spending as much time with Ann as I possibly could. She would probably tell you I was harassing her but in the end she fell for my charm and undoubted good looks. After all, she is only human!

Ann lived down the docks, with her parents, and her nan. Her mum and dad were obsessed with sport so that made it easy for me to get along with them. However, the docks had quite a bad reputation back in those days, so when I caught the bus to visit Ann she would meet me at the stop and walk me back there at the end of the night. It was comical. I was a big strapping lad from Grangetown but Ann insisted that she chaperone me as she didn't want anything bad to happen.

Whilst I was in the throes of puppy love, and still obsessed with sport, a lot of my friends got into music, drugs and fashion. None of those things pushed my buttons. Some people in the Sixties classed themselves as either a mod or a rocker and I suppose if anything I would have been a mod, purely because I couldn't afford a motorbike, which was the prerequisite of being a rocker. My only real allegiance to the mod lifestyle, however, was my Ben Sherman shirts, which I would buy from a shop in the market, when I had the money.

Music was a big thing at the time, with the Rolling Stones and the Beatles in their prime, and while I was a fan of their music the first record I bought was by Ken Dodd. The 1960s may have been a life-changing decade for some but it passed me by. All I cared about was football. By my teenage years I had started to develop into a decent little footballer who was one of the better players at school. Despite this, no club, or representative team, seemed to take any notice of me. More than anything in the world I wanted to be a professional footballer. There wasn't a lot else I aspired to, but I was beginning to worry that perhaps it was just a pipedream, particularly when friends of mine, like Jimmy Hobby, were getting picked for the Cardiff City and Cardiff Schools representative teams and no one gave me a second look.

It wasn't until I turned fourteen that I finally managed to break into the Cardiff Schools team; in part, I'm sure, because Mr Evans harassed the selectors. Cardiff Schools was a good side with a number of players who would go on to join professional clubs. Alongside me were Jimmy Hobby and Richard Newbury, who both later joined Cardiff City, and Geoff Johnston and Peter Aitken, who went on to sign for Bristol Rovers. Playing at a higher level, and with better players, didn't faze me. In fact it actually served to make me play better. I was never one to worry; I took everything in my stride and dealt with situations as I found them.

My performances for Cardiff Schools must have been reasonably impressive as they caught the attention of the Welsh selectors. One day Mr Evans told me that I had been selected for the Wales under-15 squad for the forthcoming Victory Shield tournament. I was stunned.

I had only just broken into the Cardiff Schools team, and Cardiff City had yet to take much notice of me, so to get a call up for Wales was a real surprise. With the incredible news running around in my head I sprinted home to tell my parents, who were of course thrilled. Mum was so proud that she must have told everyone she met that I was going to play for Wales.

The Victory Shield tournament was a big deal back then. All the home nations took part and it seemed that the whole country would be talking about it. Schools from all over used to take their pupils to games and this meant that most of the stadiums were full. I had attended a few of the Victory Shield games when I was younger and found it hard to believe I would be playing in them myself.

Two games that really stand out in my memory were the matches against England. The first game we played against them was at Ninian Park. What a thrill it was playing for my country at the ground of the team I had grown up supporting. All my family and friends were there giving me plenty of encouragement and I was so filled up with pride that I ran my socks off, covering every blade of grass, doing my utmost to ensure England didn't beat us in my backyard. We managed to draw the game, which was a good result, but what I will always remember is the moment our keeper, Paul Hyatt, went into a tackle with an England forward and such was the ferocity of the challenge that the ball burst!

The return match against England was played at Wembley, an experience that blew my mind. Having watched the FA Cup final year in year out I had always dreamed of one day playing at that stadium and it certainly lived up to my expectations. From driving up Wembley Way, seeing the Twin Towers loom large in front of me, and running onto a pitch that resembled a bowling green, was just fabulous.

Unbelievably, around one hundred thousand people were in the stadium and the screams from the school kids made it feel as if we were playing at a pop concert. As I was stood in the tunnel, waiting to walk out onto the pitch, I swear that the noise was so loud I could feel the floor vibrate. The intense atmosphere may have unsettled a few of our lads, as we did not play anywhere near our potential and ended up losing 3–1. I probably spent more time staring in amazement at my surroundings than concentrating on the match. Although we didn't perform particularly well I still have fond memories of playing at Wembley. What an experience for a kid.

Despite playing for Wales, scouts from clubs weren't beating down my door to sign me. I began to think that maybe it was not to be. However, just as I was losing heart, Harry Parsons, of Cardiff City, came to my house one evening and asked if I was interested in attending a few training sessions with the youth team. Was I interested? You bet your life I was. Every Tuesday night, after school, I would make my way over to Jubilee Park – which was opposite Ninian Park – to train. A lot of the guys used to call it 'Dog Shit Park' and it didn't take me long to work out why, because after a session we would be covered in the stuff. We didn't moan though, everyone just got on with it. Every training session was do-or-die for me. I had to work twice as hard as everyone else if I was going to make it. There were players who were technically better than I was, so I knew I had to make up for it through guts, determination and sheer hard work.

Harry Parsons would usually be at training and I soon learned what a great character he was. Always jovial, permanently smiling and with a good word to say about everyone, Harry was the life-blood of Cardiff City during my time at the club. His personality matched his size; he was a big bloke, larger than life. No one loved a joke more than Harry. He was always having a laugh and he would have done anything that the club wanted. In fact in his time there he did everything, from being a scout, trainer, physio and kitman to general dogsbody.

One of Harry's main jobs was looking after the storeroom, which doubled up as his office. That was where the club kept the spare kit and boots, which the players could request if theirs had worn out. You had no chance of getting into that room without his permission and you really had to push hard to persuade him that your kit needed replacing.

Visiting Harry in the storeroom was like going to see your head-master. You would knock on his door and wait to be invited in. Once inside you would plead your case. Your boots could have big holes in them, or the sole could have come off, but that wouldn't guarantee a new pair. Whatever the problem he would suggest you try superglue.

There would be a big hole in your training top and he would still say, 'Have you tried superglue?' If you had miraculously managed to move him with your plight he would say that you would then have to ask the manager, Jimmy Scoular, for his approval. As I will later explain, getting anything out of Jimmy Scoular was a miracle in itself.

A prank we loved playing on Harry was when he had his physio hat on at youth games. If one of us went down injured he would lumber onto the pitch, with his bucket of water and his magic sponge. As he was such a big guy, by the time he reached us, he would be sweating profusely and breathing heavily. Knowing this, sometimes we would go down on the far side of the pitch, which meant he had further to run to get to us. Just as he reached us we would get up and tell him everything was all right. He would turn the air blue with his language, and we would be in stitches as he bumbled back to the sidelines muttering under his breath.

Back in those days our youth-team games would be played at either Coronation or Corinthian Park (which used to be on Llandaff Road, but has since been replaced by houses). If we were lucky we would play at the sports centre at Guest Keen's, on Sloper Road, a fantastic development that boasted a clubhouse, tennis courts, cricket pitch, as well as top-notch football facilities. Unfortunately Guest Keen's is no more, as it too became another victim of the developers.

Putting on that blue Cardiff shirt sent shivers down my spine. It was identical to the shirt the first team wore and I felt out of this world playing in it. For me that was as good as it got. Although I was now part of the youth set up, playing for the first team still seemed an impossible dream. In fact, I was so sure I wasn't going to be offered terms at the club that I had virtually agreed to undertake a carpentry apprenticeship down at the docks. My brother-in-law, Derrick, was working there and he said that if I was interested he would look after me. I was just about to leave school, with no qualifications, and my dream of playing for Cardiff seemed to be fading away, so a secure job sounded good.

However, just as I turned sixteen, and was about to sign the apprenticeship forms, Harry Parsons asked to see me in his office at Ninian Park. Inside, waiting for me, was not only Harry but also Lew Clayton, who was one of the trainers, and Lance Haywood, who was club secretary. I was offered two years on the ground staff for the grand sum of £5 8s 4d per week (£5.42 in today's money). Getting paid for the privilege to play for Cardiff was a bonus; I would have played for free. I was so excited I stopped listening to anything else they may have said after that; I just wanted to sign the contract before they changed their minds. There were no agents in those days either. You took what you were offered and considered yourself lucky.

It was one of the happiest days of my life. I remember rushing back to the flat in Grangetown and excitedly telling my parents. They were of course concerned that I was turning down a good opportunity with the carpentry apprenticeship, but they understood that this was my dream, and were made up for me. I couldn't believe my luck. Just as it seemed I was facing life as a carpenter I still had a chance of one day walking out at Ninian Park as a Cardiff City player. It scarcely seemed possible.

# 3

# Learning the Ropes

My two years on the ground staff at Cardiff City were great but it was bloody hard work. Not only did we train our guts out – in the hope that by the time we reached our eighteenth birthday we would be offered a pro contract – but we were also used as slave labour. No matter how disgusting a job was we did it with a smile on our faces. I certainly didn't complain because I was just thrilled to be playing alongside my heroes.

Just a few months previously I had been watching my idols as a fan on the Grange End, but now, as a sixteen-year-old, I was getting a chance to play with them every day. At the time the big stars in the first team were Don Murray, Brian Clark, Peter King, Ronnie Bird, Ian Gibson, Mel Sutton, John Toshack, Brian Harris and Bobby Woodruff. For a club that was only in the second division it was a very talented squad.

Ronnie Bird was a great laugh; he really was the heart and soul of the changing room. He loved a joke and was always on the go, cooking up a prank, or dishing out nicknames in his high-pitched voice. Sometimes he would go too far, and as he was so small, no one thought twice about giving him a slap.

Despite Birdy being the one who usually gave out nicknames he didn't come up with mine. One day Fred Davies, the first-team goal-keeper, remarked that I looked like the Everton forward, Joe Royle. From that moment on everyone at the club called me 'Joe' and the name has stuck. There are certainly worse nicknames, and I don't mind it at all, but my wife isn't too pleased when people use it.

Birdy's partner in crime would usually be Brian Harris, who we called 'Hooky'. Hooky had arrived at Cardiff after winning the FA Cup with Everton and he really was top drawer. Sometimes he could be very serious, but he could also be the ultimate wind-up artist and as a result we never knew how to take him. His favourite trick was making something up, such as tartan paint, and then asking one of the apprentices to go to the shop to get it for him. You never knew whether he was pulling your leg, but if you protested he would bollock you, so more often than not you would go. When you returned empty handed, feeling like a pillock, you would be greeted by the sight of Hooky crying with laughter.

I'll always remember the time when Harry Parsons caddied for Hooky during a round of golf. Hooky sliced his shot into what looked like a bunker and he asked poor Harry to get it out of there for him. As Harry stepped into the 'bunker' he sank all the way up to his waist! It was actually a bog and as poor Harry tried desperately to clamber out Hooky was on his knees in hysterics.

As you can tell, Hooky was a real character. I remember Gary Bell telling me that, at night, in order for him to sneak to the pub without his wife finding out, he would tell her he was going for a run. As soon as he was out of the door he would jump in his car and take off the handbrake so it would roll down the hill without making a noise. He would only start it up when it was too far away for his better half to hear the engine!

Training with all those characters meant that most days I couldn't wait to get started. In fact I was usually one of the first to arrive at Ninian Park. Up by eight, quick wash, grab something to eat and then I would run to the ground. Only the manager, Jimmy Scoular, or Harry Parsons, would be in before me. When the apprentices arrived at the ground we were assigned jobs to carry out before the pros came in. The plum job was being in charge of the kit and everyone was after it. When I first arrived at Cardiff, Brian Rees had the assignment so I had to make do with other less glamorous chores. However, when Brian became a pro himself I was lucky enough to bag the kit job, much to the envy of my teammates.

The training kit for the players was, however, far removed from the sponsored, state-of-the-art stuff you get today. Back then it was all old gear, some of it with holes in, and most of the socks didn't match. No one moaned though, because we didn't know any better. The one drawback would be when it rained, and the kit would be sodden and filthy. The club didn't launder the kit for the players, and no one would take it home with them, so it would be left to me to dry it out on radiators and boilers around Ninian Park. The musty stench would be horrible, and you had no chance of getting the mud off, as the kit was stained a permanent sludge colour. You were supposed to wear jerseys that went with your squad number but it was impossible to tell which piece of kit was yours as the numbers were covered in layers of mud, which had accumulated over the years.

Once the pros arrived, and had changed, Jimmy Scoular took us for training. In those days, the first team, reserves, Welsh League side and the schoolboys would all train together. Jimmy hated anyone else coaching his teams; he was a real control freak. It was either do things his way or you packed your bags. In fact the only person at the club who would stand up to him was Harry Parsons, and I think he only got away with it because he made Jimmy laugh.

Jimmy Scoular was a craggy Scot with an unbelievable determination to win at all costs. In his time as a pro he made over six hundred Football League appearances for the likes of Portsmouth (where he won the league twice), Newcastle (where he won the FA Cup) and Bradford Park Avenue. He was also capped nine times for Scotland. As well as those accolades Scoular was renowned for his uncompromising style of play. Ferocious tackling was his trademark and I have heard that the Manchester United superstar, Duncan Edwards, once said that Jimmy was the hardest player he had ever seen. In fact some reports make the point that he played as though he hated everyone else on the field, demolishing opponents, bawling-out teammates and confronting referees. At times he managed that way too!

He certainly brought his wholehearted playing style into management and the youngsters, as well as some of the senior pros, were terrified of him. When he was concentrating on football he was so intense. If you didn't follow his instructions to the letter he would tear strips off you. I remember seeing senior pros in tears after Scoular had laid into them for not doing as they were told. For some reason he never really picked on me, probably because as a schoolboy I just kept my head down and worked as hard as I could. In my mind Scoular was the boss, and had much more experience of professional football than me. If he told me to jump I would ask how high.

Scoular's training sessions were hell. Almost everything we did focussed on building up stamina, particularly in pre-season. During those summer months we barely saw a ball, we ran until we dropped, and when we dropped we were told just how useless we were. Usually we would start off at Ninian Park, run all the way to Leckwith Hill, and then the few miles onto Dinas Powys. Once we were there we would do an array of exercises, such as doggies. They were horrendous. You would have cones set out in front of you, about five yards apart. We would have to run five yards and back, ten yards and back, fifteen yards and back and so on, all while being timed. Scoular would have us doing doggies until we puked. Nor did he miss anything; he was like a hawk. If you ever tried to cheat during training he would go ballistic. In the end the players realised it just wasn't worth it.

Following our doggies hell we would then have to run back to Ninian Park in a set time. I wasn't the best long-distance runner, so I would really struggle with it, but I did my best to ensure that I kept within the time set by Scoular. If you did go over the limit there would be hell to pay. Sometimes he would make you do the run again.

Mel Sutton and Les Lee actually enjoyed the running. The two of them were so skinny they looked as if a breeze could blow them over, but they could run all day long. Speaking of Les Lee reminds me of a funny story that Don Murray told me. Don said that after one game he was in the players bar and Les complained that he was going to be sick. Just before he emptied his stomach Don grabbed an empty box, which was on the bar, and gave it to Les. Unfortunately, the box didn't have a bottom and Les was sick all over himself!

Another of Scoular's favourite pre-season runs started at the bottom of the Wenault. He would have us run to the top, do more doggies and then run back down again. On our return to the ground he would sometimes have us run around the track at Ninian Park. Standing at the finishing line, he would be waiting with his stopwatch. In order to avoid a tongue lashing you had to ensure you made the time, sometimes at the expense of your teammates. The track around Ninian Park was only a couple of yards wide so only a few of you could go at a time. Going around the final corner, if you weren't in the lead, you would sometimes have to bump the person next to you out of the way, so that you wouldn't be held up. Your mate wouldn't be best pleased but it was worth it to avoid one of the manager's infamous dressing downs.

Scoular was so obsessed by physical fitness that he would even slog us to death on the Friday before a game. He would have us doing leapfrog and sprints and by the end of it your legs would be so heavy you wondered whether you would be in a fit state to play the next day.

However, not putting in 100 per cent during a match wasn't an option under Jimmy. If you shirked anything he would blow his top. Losing a game was a fate worse than death. You would do your best to avoid him as he would take out his frustrations on anyone he encountered. He would have us back in for training on the Sunday and would subject us to more running. It was hell at times but it certainly made us fit. If we won a game, however, Scoular would be all smiles, cracking jokes in the changing room, and asking how you and the family were doing. He certainly kept you on your toes.

During the season, if we behaved, we would usually end training with a game of five-a-side. You would have thought that we would have been delighted to actually play with a ball, but you would be wrong. The teams were chosen by picking squad numbers that were written on the back of bottle tops, out of a plastic bag. If you were picked to be on Scoular's team your heart would sink. You had to win at all costs or face humiliation. Those five-a-side games could be hell. He would run his bollocks off, and scream at you until he was blue in the face. I was from a working-class background, and bad language never fazed me, but some of the things Scoular screamed even made me cringe. In fact, when we trained at Jubilee Park, such was the volcanic nature of his expletive-laden tantrums that local residents actually petitioned the club to stop us training there. Jubilee Park is of course a public park, but no one from the council ever tried physically to kick us off it. I dread to think what would have happened if someone had tried it with Scoular there.

I vividly remember this five-a-side game in which Bill Harvey, the reserve-team trainer, was in goal for Scoular's side. At one point the ball went out of play, near Bill's goal, so he went to fetch it, unaware that the game had continued with a new ball. While Bill was out of the goal the opposing team scored the winner. Scoular went nuts and sacked poor Bill on the spot. Bill was told to pack his bags and to never set foot in the club again. All over a goal in five-a-side game! After cooling off Scoular saw sense, and Bill was allowed to return, but as a young kid it certainly made you think that if you ever made the slightest mistake the manager would have no hesitation in sacking you.

Because of Jimmy's attitude I always made sure that during the five-a-side games I gave everything I had. I don't think it went down particularly well with some of the senior pros, as I would be lunging into all sorts of tackles, but it had to be done so that the manager would pick on someone other than me. At one point Brian Clark complained to Scoular that I was going in too hard, which saw him told, in no uncertain terms, to stop being a girl. It was probably because I was so committed in those games that Scoular warmed to me. Although he let rip at others he always seemed to lay off me.

Scoular was still a very good player. He must have been in his forties, but he was as fit as a fiddle and physically he seemed massive. I remember he had huge thighs, which enabled him to hit the ball like a rocket. His speciality was thundering a ball from one side of the pitch to the other, with no discernible effort. The receiving player would wince as the ball came towards him, chest height, as it would sting when it made contact.

After we had finished training everyone would go back to Ninian Park for a bath in the changing room. The bath was huge, and could easily accommodate most of the team, so we all used to wash in there together. Looking back it was horrible. The water would be black, and the sides would be caked in mud, but no one cared, we just jumped in. Scoular would usually be in there with us and he was a totally different person away from the training field. Telling jokes, regaling us with stories, and asking how we were. He came across as a lovely bloke, despite the fact that just minutes before he had been a bear with a sore head.

In those days the atmosphere among the lads was great and I loved being part of it. The first-team boys were always as good as gold, but

I used to spend the majority of my time with the rest of the ground staff: the likes of John Williams, Alan Couch, Alan Shaw, Jimmy Hobby, Nigel Rees and a guy from Aberdare called Peter Davies. When Peter first arrived at the club I don't think he had ever been outside Aberdare before and I remember that when he was asked his name he would always answer 'Peter Davies, Aberdare'.

When the pros went home after training we still had jobs to do. For instance, on Mondays, after a weekend game, we would have to clean the Grange End. Back then the Grange End was made primarily of wood, and rubbish always used to accumulate under the slats. It was a real hazard because if the stand had caught fire it would have gone up in no time at all. Getting down on our stomachs we would crawl under the slats to clean out the crap, which meant we got absolutely filthy. Our faces would be black, and when we sneezed the snot would look like tar. While the job was disgusting it could also be profitable as occasionally we would find money that the fans had dropped.

Scoular was fanatical about us not only doing our jobs to perfection but also completing them according to his timetable. When that time had arrived he would come out of his office and closely inspect our efforts. God help you if they weren't up to scratch. If there was still a speck of dirt in the bath, or if the stands hadn't been swept adequately, he would call you every name under the sun and make the whole youth team stay behind until the job had been according to his exacting specifications.

It wouldn't surprise me if Scoular had obsessive-compulsive disorder. Everything had to be just right. One summer's day he asked our groundsman, Keith, to mow the pitch by 4.00 p.m. Keith had a motorised petrol lawnmower, which you sat on to mow the grass, and he was the only person who could ever get the thing to work. While he was in the middle of the job he was called away to on an urgent matter so he set off and left the mower on the pitch.

At quarter to four Scoular emerged to inspect the pitch and found the job only half done. With the prospect of the grass not being cut by the deadline he decided to roll up his sleeves and do it himself. The only problem was that he couldn't get the mower's engine going. Most people would have admitted defeat, and waited for the groundsman to come back, but that wasn't Scoular's style. In searing heat he proceeded to push this huge lawnmower up and down the pitch under his own steam until it was clipped to perfection. When Keith returned he was greeted by the sight of the manager drenched in sweat and cursing him profusely. In fact he was so angry that he told Keith to piss off while he finished the job himself.

Despite Scoular keeping us on our toes we did find the time to have a bit of fun. To keep ourselves entertained during the afternoon we would borrow the groundsman's tractors and have races around Ninian Park. Messing around on the tractors did, however, almost end in tragedy. I remember one day when Jimmy Hobby was sat in the driver's seat, while the rest of us were gathered around chatting. As Jimmy went to reverse the tractor his foot slipped, which resulted in it lurching forward. Billy Kellock had been leaning on the front wheel, but before he could move it went right over him. As soon as I saw what had happened I feared the worst. Best-case scenario, I said to myself, he would have a few broken bones, but I also thought it might have killed him. Unbelievably, Billy got straight back up, and, apart from a few bruises, he was fine. It was a lucky escape and to this day I still don't know how he got off so lightly.

Another regular amusement would see us to organise races to the top of the floodlights. The floodlights were of course massive and we would scurry up there without a safety harness. If the electrician was replacing the bulbs we loved to wind him up. One of us would stand at the bottom and shout that there was an urgent call for him. The electrician would come back down, which could take him between five and ten minutes, and then when he had reached the bottom we would tell him that the caller had hung up. I lost count of the number of times we did that, but he fell for it every time.

It sounds as if we were all permanently messing around but that youth-team squad was actually very talented and highly committed. Once we had gelled we soon had most clubs in the country sitting up and taking notice because we did something that no City youth team has achieved, either before or since.

# 4

# Making My Mark

My first year in the youth team was spent learning the ropes and getting used to what was required as a professional. It was hard work, but as the year came to a close I was satisfied with my efforts. Playing most of my football at centre back I certainly hadn't let myself down, but I also counted myself lucky that I was playing for a very capable team. As the year went on we really started to click and we destroyed most of our opponents.

In those days there wasn't a dedicated league for youth teams so we played our matches in a local amateur league. It was tough, as most of our opponents were grown men who liked nothing more than showing up the kids from Cardiff City. We had to learn how to handle ourselves because our opponents realised that if they were to have any chance of winning they had to intimidate us. In order to escape getting kicked up in the air we soon learned that we needed to move the ball quickly. Once we took that on board, and got into our stride, most teams at that level couldn't touch us and we won the league at a canter.

By 1971, my second year on the ground staff, the team had matured and I had a feeling we could really go places. John Williams was a great goalkeeper, Jimmy Hobby and I had a solid partnership at the back, and then we had the likes of Brian Rees, Jimmy McInch, Alan Couch and Derek Showers pulling the strings, putting in tackles and scoring goals. It was a nicely balanced side, and we were as close on the pitch as we were off it.

That year we entered the FA Youth Cup and managed to go further in the competition than any Cardiff City youth team had ever done before or has done since. Taking great pleasure in playing our rivals, Swansea City, off the park, we cruised through the first round after a 3–0 romp. Next up were Southampton and we put in another convincing performance, racking up four goals without reply. Plymouth, in the next round, were trickier opposition but we managed to sneak past them in a tight game that finished 3–2. In the quarter-final we faced Rotherham, but they were no match for us as we coasted to a 3–0 win. Suddenly, we found ourselves in the semi-final.

Waiting for us in the last four were Burnley, and we faced the tough prospect of having to beat them at Turf Moor if we were to progress. Managing to scrape a draw at their place we were very confident that we could turn them over in the replay at Ninian Park. That game, however, also finished in a draw, which meant we had to go back up to Burnley. I thought we may have blown our chance, but in that third game we played out of our skins and won 3–1. That night we stayed in Burnley and we went out and had a few beers. We were just so proud that we were the first Cardiff City side to reach the FA Youth final. I remember thinking that it would have to be a great team to stop us now, as we were really playing well.

The team that was aiming to stop us was the mighty Arsenal, who had conceded only one goal in the entire competition. Despite their reputation we didn't fear them. We thought we had enough to do them over, and with the second leg being at Ninian Park, I felt that it was our destiny to lift the trophy at home.

Playing at Highbury, in the first leg, was a wonderful feeling. Walking through the famous marble corridors, and seeing the bust of Herbert Chapman, gave the place a sense of grandeur and history. When I had played at Wembley, as a Wales schoolboy, the occasion had got to me, but with the experience I had gained I was able fully to focus on the game. Expecting a bombardment Jimmy Hobby and I knew we could be in for a tough night but we put in our best display of the competition. They couldn't beat us, either in the air or on the ground. The game finished goalless, which was a fantastic result, and as I left the field I was certain that glory awaited us back at Ninian Park.

Leading up to the second leg there was a lot of hype surrounding the game. All week there was heavy coverage in the local papers and fans were coming up to the youth-team boys in the street and wishing us luck. Personally, I loved it, and it gave me a taste for big-time football. On the night over twelve thousand fans turned up and the atmosphere was electric. It felt like a first-team game. Our chances had taken a slight blow beforehand due to Derek Showers, who had scored plenty of goals for us in our run to the final, being commandeered by the first team. Without our goal-scoring talisman, we knew we were facing an uphill battle, especially against the Gunners' notoriously tight defence.

I don't know if it was because of the weight of expectation, missing Derek or the fact that Arsenal played well, but we never got going. As a result we lost 2–0, which left me devastated. I had genuinely believed we would be too strong for them at home. Forty years have passed, and while I am so proud that I was a member of such a special team, that loss still hurts.

That year wasn't, however, just a special one for the youth team; it was also a memorable one for the firsts. In what is considered the greatest night in the history of the club, Cardiff City defeated European giants Real Madrid 1–0 at Ninian Park, in the European Cup Winners Cup. Regretfully, I wasn't there, as I was away playing for the Wales youth team. My teammate from the youth side, Nigel Rees, was, however, called into the squad and he actually set up the winning goal, when he raced down the wing and put in an inch-perfect cross for Brian Clark to head home. Although the boys lost the second leg in Madrid, and were knocked out of the competition, it was still an incredible feat to have beaten them in Wales.

The 1970/71 season also saw Cardiff going for promotion to the first division. Flying high, the team was playing some sparkling football, but then came what is the most controversial transfer in the history of the club: our star player, John Toshack, was transferred to Liverpool for a fee of £110,000. I think Tosh was torn, as he would have loved to have fired his hometown team into the first division but, at the same time, Liverpool were a massive club and would give him the opportunity to win trophies.

At the time a lot of our fans thought it was a scandal and many vowed never to return to Ninian Park. Tosh was of course a fan favourite, not only for his goal-scoring prowess, but also because he was born and bred in Cardiff. Many fans, and indeed some of the players, felt that selling Tosh would put an end to the promotion push and that it showed a lack of ambition. In the end Cardiff didn't make it to the top tier but would we have gone up if we had kept Tosh? We will never know for sure.

Replacing a player of Toshack's calibre was always going to be hard work and the man Scoular identified to do the job was Alan Warboys of Sheffield Wednesday. To be fair, Alan hit the ground running, scoring thirteen goals in just half a season, including four against Carlisle United – all before half time. Alan's form helped to keep the team in the promotion race and as the season neared its conclusion it looked odds on that we would go up.

With just a handful of games remaining we needed a result at promotion rivals Sheffield United. If we won we would have an excellent chance of going up, but if we lost the season was all but over. I remember that there was so much anticipation in the city as the boys made their way to Sheffield. Everyone fully expected Cardiff to win, and as a young lad on the ground staff I was excited by the thought that if we went up I would have a chance of playing in the first division.

The game was played on a weeknight and as this was before the days of Sky Sports, or even Teletext, keeping tabs on what was going on was a nightmare. Incredibly, the game wasn't even on the radio and sitting around, waiting to find out the final score, was excruciating. Sat in the living room of the family flat, with Mum and Dad, I anxiously waited for news, when, all of a sudden the final score flashed up on the screen. We had lost 5–1! What made matters even worse was that Gil Reece, who was from Grangetown, was in the Sheffield eleven and had destroyed us. It was such an anti-climax and I felt sick to my stomach.

Despite the loss against the Blades, and the youth team losing to Arsenal, there was still a sense that the club was going places. Surely with the quality players we had, and a capable manager, along with an emerging crop of highly promising youngsters, it would only be a matter of time before we were back where we belonged – in the first division.

It was a tremendously exciting time to be involved with the club and I prayed that I would be kept on as a professional. Throughout that second year on the ground staff I was looking for any kind of sign that the club was going to offer me a pro contract. Any comment from the staff, good or bad, was amplified in my mind as I tried to analyse whether it meant I would be signed or released. I honestly didn't have a clue what the club thought of me, but I couldn't bear the thought of what I would do if they decided I hadn't made the grade.

Usually, if the club thought you were up to it, they would offer you a pro contract on your eighteenth birthday. All the ground-staff boys kept track of birthdays so that we knew when to pounce. Days before the 'lucky' team-member's birthday we would gather together and plan our ambush. On the fateful day, if we saw our teammate emerge from Scoular's office with a smile on his face, we would strike. Like a pack of jackals we would grab our teammate, pin him down, shave off his pubic hair and cover him from head to toe in black shoe polish. It wasn't the most pleasant way to celebrate getting a pro contract, but it certainly gave us a laugh. The more you squealed and wriggled the worst it would get.

As my eighteenth approached I started to get butterflies in my stomach. I honestly didn't have a clue if they were going to keep me or let me go. When the big day came Jimmy Scoular called me into his office. I was so nervous I felt sick. This was the day of reckoning and I was either going to play professional football for the club I loved or join my friends working down the docks. I remember Scoular telling me to sit down, while he sat behind his desk and went over my progress. I was desperate for him to deliver the news but he seemed to enjoy dragging it out. Finally, the moment came. Looking me in the eye, he paused, and then finally said, 'Son, I'm going to take a chance on you. I'm prepared to offer you a two-year contract for £20 a week.'

Get in there!

My heart jumped out of my chest. There was no thought of trying to negotiate or tell him I needed time to think. Before he had a chance to say another word I jumped up, shook his hand and accepted the offer. I like to think that I remained cool, calm and collected, but the truth is that I probably had a big, stupid grin on my face. I was ecstatic.

When I walked out of Scoular's office I had almost forgotten about the initiation ceremony. But the lads hadn't. They watched me stagger out of Scoular's office in a happy daze and then they struck without mercy. As soon as they collared me I knew what was going to happen but I was so happy I didn't care. Unlike those who had gone before me I didn't struggle, I just let them get on with it as I was shaved and polished.

After spending ages scrubbing myself clean I made my way home to break the good news to my parents. They were of course delighted for me and they knew how worried I had been in the weeks leading up to my birthday. Ann was also thrilled, probably because I could now afford to take us somewhere other than the Black and White café!

Years later I was told by Harry Parsons that Scoular had actually come very close to letting me go. Strangely, a knee injury had made him change his mind. One day, after training, I was having a shower when all of a sudden my knee locked. I had never had any problems with my knees and didn't know what was wrong, so I banged it as hard as I could and eventually I could bend it again. Over the next few weeks the problem kept recurring and I had no option but to tell Lew Clayton about it. Lew checked me in to see the club doctor and it turned out that I had torn my cartilage. These days a cartilage operation is relatively minor, and you can be in and out of hospital within a few hours. However, back then it was quite serious, and meant that I had to spend two weeks in hospital recuperating.

Around this stage I think Scoular had told Harry he was going to let me go but decided to wait until after the operation to tell me. For whatever reason, once I regained full fitness, he changed his mind. It is certainly very odd to think that if I hadn't suffered that injury I might never have got my chance in professional football.

I was happy that I had signed a pro-contract but I knew only too well that there was a lot of hard work ahead if I was ever to break into the first team. As I have mentioned already, the team was very strong, so I realised I might have to bide my time and wait for an opportunity. Whatever happened I was determined that I would be ready when it eventually came my way.

# 5

# Good Things Come to Those Who Wait

Getting down to business, as a professional footballer, in the summer of 1971, was an enormously exciting prospect. The previous season we had beaten Real Madrid, reached the FA Youth Cup final and come agonisingly close to promotion to the first division. Everything seemed to be in place for another exciting season and I was grateful to be part of it.

You would have thought that everyone would have been buzzing but, if anything, it seemed that the club (and our fans) were suffering from a hangover. Some were still angry at the loss of Tosh; others thought we had lost our chance of getting back to the big time, and, in consequence, were a bit dispirited; while age, and loss of form, had caught up with a few.

Matters weren't helped when the club decided to sell Ronnie Bird and Brian Harris. As I mentioned in the last chapter, Brian and Ronnie were the life and soul of the dressing room, and the atmosphere changed a little once they left. Brian had also been an inspirational person to have around and the team definitely missed his leadership skills.

Far from looking forward to the new season I sensed that a few of the boys felt that it would turn into a long hard slog. They were proved right. However, at this stage I was still only a kid looking to make his way in the game and such matters didn't concern me. Being involved in the first team still seemed like a distant prospect and I just wanted to get my head down and learn as much as I could from Don Murray and the other senior players.

During the 1971/72 season I spent most of my time playing for the Welsh League team on a Saturday and then the reserves, in the Football League Combination, on a Wednesday afternoon. The Welsh League was a very good standard in those days and had a lot of former professional players, including the great Ivor Allchurch, who played for Haverfordwest. Despite Cardiff having a team packed with talent we could never rest on our laurels and had to fight for every point. We were the Welsh League's glamour boys and we invariably attracted decent crowds when we played away. Everyone wanted to beat us. At times the atmosphere in those small grounds could be intimidating, but it was a great learning experience.

Playing in the Combination League was also a steep learning curve and I noticed the step up in standard. It was full of top teams like Fulham, Spurs and Arsenal and it was great facing players I had only ever read about, or seen on television. Even though the grounds were empty it was a wonderful experience to play at stadiums like Stamford Bridge and White Hart Lane. Jimmy Scoular watched the reserve games from the stand and with the grounds being empty we could hear him curse every time we made a mistake.

Over the course of the season both the reserves and the Welsh League team won more games than they lost and in consequence finished quite high up the table. While teammates such as Rees, Kellock and Couch all got their chance in the first team I wasn't able to break into the squad. Far from being discouraged, however, I felt I had enough on my plate just learning my trade in the reserves and was happy to be making steady progress. In my heart I knew I wasn't quite ready for the first team, but hoped that if I kept going I would eventually get my chance.

Besides, if I was ever going to break into the first team I had to hope that Dave Carver, who played in my preferred position at right back, would succumb to injury or loss of form. That is the sad thing about professional football: if you're out of the side the only way you will get back in is if misfortune befalls one of your mates. Dave was, however, a very solid, dependable, full back who never gave less than 100 per cent. Scoular loved him and as a result he started ninety-three consecutive league games between 1969 and 1971. I knew that I could be facing a long wait.

The first team spent most of the 1971/72 season in a relegation battle and there were very few highlights. The one game that did get everyone excited was when we drew my boyhood heroes, Leeds United, in the FA Cup. Unfortunately, I didn't get to see Billy Bremner and co light up Ninian Park as I was playing for the Welsh League team. Predictably, Leeds, in front of 45,000 fans, were too strong for a struggling Cardiff team and came away with a convincing 2–0 win.

Having managed to avoid relegation, Jimmy Scoular attempted to mix things up during pre-season by changing the style of play. Up to that point the team had played the ball from back to front as quickly as possible but in that summer of 1972 he tried to introduce a Continental style of football. In training we focused on being patient and were told to wait for the right moment to pick a pass, rather than simply hoof it up field.

I remember that when Bill Irwin, the first-team goalkeeper, had the ball the full backs were told to hug the touchline. If they were unmarked Bill would throw the ball out to one of them. Rather than lump it down the channel, as they usually did, the full backs passed the ball along the back four until one of the midfielders dropped short and made himself available. Once a midfielder had the ball he also had to keep possession until a forward found space to receive a pass. These tactics are commonplace today, but back then they were almost unheard of and it was clear from the beginning that they were never going to work. The first problem was the pitches, many of which resembled a farmer's field. Trying to control and pass the ball accurately on them was very difficult. The result was that moves broke down in the early stages and the boys played themselves into trouble.

Disregarding the state of the pitches, in order for this approach to work, players had to feel comfortable on the ball. Most of the guys gave their all, and were as honest as they come, but they didn't have the technical skills that were necessary to execute Jimmy Scoular's master plan. Scoular would of course tear his hair out but he was being unrealistic. Players in the second division, on bobbly pitches, were unsuited to that type of silky soccer. A few of the boys grumbled and it reached the point where they just couldn't win. If they dwelt on the ball, looking for a pass, they would hear the crowd groan, urging them to leather it up the field. When they did this Scoular would go nuts at them from the sidelines. More often than not they would get caught in two minds and take stick from both the manager and the fans.

Even before Scoular's disastrous Continental football experiment the first team were facing an uphill battle as Jimmy decided to sell Brian Clark, Alan Warboys and Ian Gibson. Losing the goals that Clarkey and Warboys guaranteed was a huge blow, and Gibbo wasn't just a talented player – he was also great in the dressing room. In his defence Scoular did, however, bring in some useful replacements. Johnny Vincent, signed from Middlesbrough, was a very skilful mid-fielder, and he became a crowd favourite after scoring against his old club on his debut. Willie Anderson joined us from Aston Villa for £60,000, and was a class act. Willie had also played for Manchester United, where he had been George Best's understudy, and he had cer-tainly picked up plenty of tips from the great man, beating a man for fun and delivering fantastic crosses from the right wing. Cardiff-born Gil Reece, our tormentor at Sheffield United the previous season, was another good addition. Gil had been flying before he had broken his leg but he was still an excellent player and he led by example. As a result Scoular made him club captain and he really commanded everyone's respect.

With players coming and going, and the team unsure of how it was supposed to play, it was hardly surprising that we made a poor start to the season, winning just twice in eleven games. At the same time I was playing well for the reserves, and for the Welsh League team, and felt confident that I was ready for bigger things. Dave Carver had not started the season at his best and I sensed that if things continued in this manner I might get my chance sooner rather than later.

One Friday afternoon I remember scanning the team sheets – which were posted on the changing-room wall at Ninian Park – and found that my name wasn't listed in the Welsh League side. Quickly scouring the other lists I did a double take when I saw that I was the last name on the sheet for the first-team squad, who were due to face QPR the next day. Although I wasn't in the starting eleven, or even a sub, I would still be travelling with the squad. Should one of the boys come down with an injury, or illness, before the game, I would take my place on the bench. Just to be a part of the day was a huge bonus, and while I realised that I was unlikely to see any action, it was good to know I was on the manager's radar.

Though I didn't even get out of my suit for the match I will always remember standing in the player's tunnel, before the game, alongside QPR's star man, Stan Bowles. With just fifteen minutes to kickoff, Stan's teammates were warming up but he was still in his suit. He refused to move until he knew the result of a big race that he had wagered a lot of money on! I'd like to see modern players pull that stunt with the managers of today.

As I said it was great being with the first team, but the lads were no match for QPR, who strolled to a 3–0 win. Scoular did his nut after the game and I could see that the pressure was beginning to get to him. The team were at the wrong end of the table and the next game, against Leyton Orient at Brisbane Road, promised to be another tough encounter. Something had to change and I hoped it might be the opportunity I had been waiting for.

During the week I began to think that I had a good chance of once again making the squad. Dave Carver had struggled against QPR and I thought I could do no worse. When the squad was named on the Friday I was hoping to make the bench, but I was stunned to see that I was the second name on the list. I was starting! Without hesitating I ran straight home to tell my parents and to ring Ann. Everyone was made up for me.

On the coach to London I don't mind admitting that I was a little nervous. This was the chance I had been waiting for and I knew I couldn't afford to blow it. Don Murray settled me down by telling me to play my natural game and he would help me through. At least I knew that should I make a mistake I had Don alongside me to clean up the mess. In the changing room before the game the lads all wished me good luck and as I walked out of the room Scoular patted me on the back and gave me a wink. There was no way I was going to let him down. This was what I had been waiting for.

When I stepped out onto the pitch I was determined to give everything I had. This was my dream, playing for my hometown club, and I knew that such opportunities don't come around too often. You have to make the most of them or spend the rest of your life with regrets. When I heard my name announced over the tannoy the fans gave me a cheer, which really psyched me up. Seeing the number of fans who had made the journey inspired me. If I hadn't made the grade at Cardiff I would have been one of them and I knew how much getting a result meant to them.

The game was always going to be difficult for a young debutant in a struggling team, particularly when I had to mark Ian Bowyer, who had scored a hat-trick against us the previous season. Matters certainly weren't helped when Alan Foggan was sent off after half an hour, leaving us with ten men and facing an Orient onslaught. But despite attack after attack we held firm, with Don helping me no end with my positioning. Orient's Ian Broadbent, who also happened to be high up in the PFA, was causing us a few problems at one point so Don ordered me to sort him out. With Don's words ringing in my ear I proceeded to kick him into the stands. 'Who the hell is this kid?' Ian moaned to Don, 'Doesn't he know I represent him with the PFA?' Next time he had the ball I made sure I kicked him even harder for whining, much to the delight of Don, who patted me on the backside as I strode past him, full of confidence.

Although we only had ten men for most of the game we came away from Brisbane Road with a goalless draw. The atmosphere in the changing room afterwards was buoyant and for once Jimmy Scoular seemed satisfied. Even though he didn't say anything to me about my performance I must have done reasonably well because I was in the team for the next game, against high-flying Middlesbrough.

For years I had gone to Ninian Park as a fan, and had played reserve-team games there, but the feeling I got in my first start for the top team, striding out onto that pitch, was incredible. It was everything I had hoped it would be and more. As the energy of the fans pulsated onto the pitch everything swirled around in my head: the smell of burgers and Bovril; the roof on the Bob Bank advertising Captain Morgan rum; the incessant twirling of scarves and rattles amidst chants and jeers. It had my heart beating faster than I ever thought possible. 'Phil,' I thought to myself, 'there's no doubt about it, you're in heaven.'

When Johnny Vincent put us in front I felt as if I was in the middle of a tornado, such was the din the crowd made. Cheering as a fan, in a packed stand, was one thing, but watching the celebrations as a player, in the middle of the pitch, was something else. Gary Bell stroked home a penalty to make it 2–0 and that sealed not only a tremendous victory but also a home debut I had long dreamed about.

Walking off the Ninian Park pitch, waving to my family and Ann, who were in the Grand Stand, I was on top of the world. Everyone who mattered to me was at the game and I had given it everything. I wanted that moment to last forever. I felt invincible.

From that moment on I was a fixture in the team, but I knew I couldn't afford to get cocky. One slip could see me back where I had started and after having a taste of being a winner on a professional football pitch, I was eager for more. One thing that really pleased me was how the Cardiff fans seemed to immediately take to me. I always felt they were on my side and wanted me to do well. I admit I wasn't the most skilful player in the world, but I loved a tackle, and always gave my best, and I think the fans appreciated that side of my game. It used to fill me with pride when I heard them singing 'Six foot two, eyes of blue, Joey Dwyer's after you.'

The second division was full of top teams that year, such as Aston Villa, Sunderland and Nottingham Forest, and I used to love visiting their grounds. Walking out at stadiums such as Villa Park, Roker Park and the City Ground made me feel like a big-time footballer. However, one ground that most players were never keen on visiting was Millwall's stadium, the Den. It was a nasty and intimidating place to go, with the fans right on top of you, baying for blood. To be honest I was in my element when we played there. The more the crowd got on my back the better I played and we came away with a hard-earned point.

Our form throughout the season was very patchy. Following great wins, over teams such as Middlesbrough, we would contrive to lose 3–0 to the likes of Burnley. Such was our inconsistency that it looked to all and sundry that we would be going down but with just a few games left we pulled off a great 4–1 win against Huddersfield, in which Andy McCulloch scored a brilliant solo goal to set us on our way. That win gave us a fighting chance, and with the penultimate game of the season at home to Sunderland we knew that our fate was in our own hands. All we needed was a solitary point and we would be safe.

Sunderland had caused a major upset the week before by beating first division Leeds United to win the FA Cup and unsurprisingly they were on a high. I think we all hoped that a tough game at Ninian Park was the last thing they would want after the drama of Wembley. To honour their historic achievement we gave Sunderland a guard of honour as they strode onto the pitch. Outside we were all smiles, and full of respect, but inside we were raring to go. Scoular had worked us up into a frenzy. There was no way we were going down in front of our own fans. By the time kickoff came around I was like a wild animal let out of a cage and from the first minute I was launching myself into tackles as if my life depended on it. Far from being the only one who was ready to fight to the death, my fellow defenders, Don Murray, Leighton Phillips and Gary Bell were also putting their bodies on the line. All of us scrapped to the death that day as we managed to secure the point we needed through a Bobby Woodruff goal, which made the final score 1–1.

Although we had done what we had set out to do the mood was far from celebratory. Yes, we were relieved, but we knew that finishing in twentieth place was hardly a cause for celebration. Such was Scoular's foul mood you would have thought we had lost ten–nil when we got back to the changing room. He was a winner through and through and he despised spending a season scrapping for our lives rather than being in contention for trophies.

It should have come as no surprise that we struggled that season as we were clearly in a transitional period. Experienced pros such as Ronnie Bird, Brian Harris, Brian Clark and Alan Warboys proved hard to replace and the team was littered with untried youngsters such as Derek Showers, Alan Couch and me. There was no doubt in my mind that we still had plenty of talent, and that perhaps with a few signings, and a bit more experience for the younger players, we had the makings of a team who could get promoted.

Despite having a poor season in the league it ended on a high when I secured my first piece of silverware as a Cardiff player when we won the Welsh Cup, beating Bangor City 5–0. The Welsh Cup was a relatively important competition back then and we were delighted not only to have won it but also to have secured European football for the following season. Watching European games, under the Ninian Park lights, had enthralled me as a fan and I couldn't wait to taste the occasion as a player.

Though it hadn't been the best of seasons for the team I was chuffed to bits with my own progress. I could hardly believe that I was now a regular for my hometown team and felt that I hadn't let anyone down. If anything I was surprised at how easily I had coped.

Everything on the pitch had gone better than I had dared hope and it turned out to be a pretty good year off it as well. Ann and I had been virtually inseparable over the previous few years and I knew that I wanted to spend the rest of my life with her. She used to watch most of the games I played at Ninian Park, in the company of her family, and after the match we would all go back to Grangetown together. Walking home after a game certainly gave me an insight into the mood of our fans. Most of them didn't recognise me and while it was nice to hear the occasional complimentary comment I also heard my fair share of criticism. It was a great way to stay in touch with the paying public.

One night, as we all walked home after a draw against Swindon, I finally plucked up the courage to ask Ann's father, Frank, if I could marry his daughter. Frank was a huge Cardiff fan, and would probably have given me anything that I asked for, so he was only too happy to say yes. With Frank's blessing Ann and I didn't waste much time and within a few months we were married at St Patrick's church in Grangetown. It was a great occasion, with all the old gang from my schooldays attending, and some of the lads from the club as well. We had our reception at the old Central hotel, at the top of St Mary Street, where Frank put on a free bar, which he lived to regret as the boys took full advantage.

The best man was my City sidekick, Gary Bell, who I had grown close to during my time at the club. When Gary and his wife went out he would ask Ann and me to babysit for him, probably because we were cheap! He's a top lad Belly, but if anyone ever sees him buy a pint let me know as it's an occasion worth marking. It takes a spanner to get fifty pence out of his hand!

Once Ann and I were married we expected to move into one of the houses that the club rented to players. In those days many clubs had a significant property portfolio, but when David Goldstone took over Cardiff City he decided to sell most of the houses to raise money. At first I panicked, as I didn't think we would have anywhere to live, but thankfully the club kept a flat for us in Cowbridge Road. It was a big place, with six rooms, and all for just £5 a week.

Marriage meant that I had to become more domesticated and I suppose it made me grow up. Before tying the knot I would usually have joined the boys after training for a spot of food at the Black and White café, which would be followed by a few frames of snooker. However, now that I was married, and Ann had to work – as a receptionist at the Angel hotel – I usually had to cut short my afternoons of leisure and get back to clean the flat and put the tea on. I was a house husband way before the term was even invented!

After getting married and becoming a householder, I felt it was time that I bought my first car. 'Luckily' my brother, Brian, had an old banger he seemed very keen for me to have at a 'bargain' price. He definitely saw me coming! I remember Ann and I once drove down the motorway to see some friends in High Wycombe and I really don't know how we got there without the car falling apart. Smoke was coming out of the bonnet, the seats rocked back and forth and the car shook like a rattle the whole way there. We were terrified.

Despite driving a motor that even Del Boy would have turned his nose up at I couldn't complain about how my year had gone. It had been a success on and off the pitch and I was looking forward to the new season as an established first-team player.

# 6

# Chopping and Changing

Birmingham City kicked off our pre-season preparations in 1973 and that game also marked the opening of the new grandstand. Previously, the grandstand at Ninian Park consisted of just a small covered stand, in the middle of the open terraces, but now the cover stretched right the way across. It certainly looked very grand, but, unfortunately, our performances on the pitch were far from it.

We were given the run around by Birmingham and although there was no shame in losing to them, as they were a very capable team, the warning signs were clear. With us struggling the previous season it was obvious to everyone that changes needed to be made. Unsurprisingly, Scoular decided to clear the decks and he released some of the younger players, guys he didn't think would make the grade, such as Jimmy Hobby, Alan Couch and Billy Kellock.

It was sad to see some of my good mates leave the club, especially as we had joined at the same time and had been very close. Seeing Jimmy Hobby leave was a bit of a shock as throughout our childhood he had always been picked ahead of me. It was another wake-up call, reminding me that my position was still not safe and that if I took my foot off the gas I could soon be joining some of my youth-team pals on the scrapheap.

One thing that did happen that summer – which showed me I was still very much in Scoular's plans – was that when I reported for training I was told to change in the home dressing room at Ninian Park. In those days only the first team got changed in there, while the reserves and youth-team boys had to use the away dressing room. It was only a small thing but it certainly boosted my confidence and made me feel part of the team.

Before the start of the season I had been expecting an influx of new players particularly when Jimmy, Alan and Billy were released, but for some reason only one signing materialised, that of George Smith, from Middlesbrough. George was an experienced player, who had been around, and I think Jimmy brought him in to add a bit of knowhow. In my eyes however we definitely needed more reinforcements if we were going to have a successful season.

As I mentioned in the previous chapter, when David Goldstone took over the football club he tried to cut costs where he could, and selling the club houses had been part of that. David was a shrewd businessman and when he came in we were in dire straits financially so he looked at every single angle where he could save the club money. Unfortunately, that affected Scoular's transfer budget and I don't think David quite realised just how many players needed to be added to the squad if we were to remain competitive.

Although I thought that we needed strengthening no one seemed to moan and we just got on with the job. This approach served us well at the start of the season as we went four games unbeaten and even stuffed Oxford United 5–0. I began to think I had been wrong about the team and that maybe we had an outside chance of a promotion push. We weren't conceding many goals, and Tony Villars, Andy McCulloch and Willie Anderson looked great going forward. If we could have kept up that form, and avoided injuries, then maybe, just maybe, we had a chance.

After the Oxford game we made the trip to Selhurst Park to play the league's glamour club, Crystal Palace. Malcolm Allison was their manager and he was regarded as a brash playboy who was partial to good-looking women, cigars and champagne. Aren't we all though? Malcolm was also a media personality and everything he said made headlines. Every team in the division saw Palace as the prime scalp and we were determined to turn them over and wipe the smug smile off Allison's cocky face.

In spite of our best intentions we started the game appallingly and let Palace take a 2–0 lead. At one stage they looked as though they were going to run riot but we dug deep and an own goal brought us back into the game. Shortly afterwards Palace scored again, which led to Malcolm lighting up a huge victory cigar in the dugout. That only served to wind us up and in a dramatic finish to the match we drew level via goals from Bobby Woodruff and Johnny Vincent. It had been a great contest and I was delighted we had shown such guts and character. In my mind there was no doubt about it: we had the credentials to do very well in this league.

Around this time we also got a good draw in the Cup Winners Cup, coming up against Portuguese giants Sporting Lisbon. We drew 0–0 at Ninian Park and I couldn't wait to play in the second leg at Lisbon's famous Stadium of Light in front of fifty thousand fans. The Stadium of Light was one of Europe's famous arenas and was everything I hoped it would be. The bowl-shaped stands wrapped around the pitch, which helped to trap the noise of the fervent fans. Everything was pristine, compared to ramshackle Ninian Park, and it gave off a vibe of ambition and success. Although we lost the second leg 2–1, we did ourselves proud, and it was a real thrill to play in such a fantastic atmosphere.

By this stage we were fifth in the table, and everything seemed to be shaping up nicely, but then, out of nowhere, we collapsed. Aston Villa proceeded to murder us 5–0 on a day that we couldn't do anything right. Even Bobby Woodruff somehow managed to score an own goal, from forty yards – and with his head! Over the course of the next five games we only won once and soon our early-season form was a distant memory as we nosedived down the table.

Scoular was taking his frustration out on everyone. At times I thought he was going to have a heart attack, particularly after we lost 4–2 to Oxford just weeks after beating them 5–0. On the third of November we lost 1–0 at home to West Brom and dropped dangerously close to the relegation spots. Then, on the Monday morning, when I got in for training, I was told that the manager had been sacked. I was staggered. I realised that over the last eighteen months results hadn't been very good but in my eyes Jimmy Scoular was untouchable.

Some of the players were glad to see the back of him, but others, me included, were distraught. Jimmy gave me my chance as a professional footballer and he had stuck with me through thick and thin. Unlike some other players he never seemed to have it in for me and looking back I think he may have seen a little of himself in my playing style. There was no doubt he was a hard, stubborn bloke, who some found hard to warm to, but I thought that he was a great man manager who got everyone to give 100 per cent for the cause.

I wanted to thank him before he left so I knocked on his office door. After a short wait, with no response, I knocked again, but again there was no reply. Feeling not a little apprehension I inched my way into the room and was greeted by the sight of Jimmy, slumped in his chair, staring blankly ahead. When he saw me he tried to put on a brave face but I could tell that he was a broken man. For him failure was simply not an option and I don't think he could accept that the board had sacked him. He truly believed that he was Cardiff City Football Club. I got very emotional seeing him like that. After shaking his hand, and wishing him all the best, I found it hard to say goodbye.

In the end I think that he had worked himself into the ground and needed a rest. He used to do everything at the club; he was, if truth be told, a control freak. At first his approach had worked perfectly, but he got so immersed in the job it became damaging to his health. After Cardiff City, Jimmy took a break from management and worked as a scout for a few years. I think even he realised that he was burnt out and was probably glad to be away from the pressure-cooker environment.

With Jimmy gone, our physio, Lew Clayton, took over as care-taker manager, while the board looked for a replacement. Lew was never going to get the job on a permanent basis, but we all liked him, and gave him our best for the games he was in charge, which were against Millwall, Luton and Middlesbrough. Despite our best efforts, it wasn't enough, as we didn't win a single match, with the 3–0 loss to Middlesbrough representing a new low. It was obvious that the board needed to appoint a new manager to steady the ship before it was too late.

The players were pleasantly surprised when we heard that ex Manchester United manager, Frank O'Farrell, was going to be our new boss. Frank was a big fish for Cardiff City and I was very happy to have the chance to play for him. I hoped that I would learn a thing or two. As is always the case when a new manager comes in, you are keen to work with him, but also a bit nervous. If they don't fancy you it could mean being left out of the side and then being out of a job. After working so hard to break into the top team I was worried that he might want to bring someone in to replace me, but fortunately Frank played me from the start and stuck with me.

A key addition to Frank's backroom staff was Spurs coach, Jimmy Andrews, who had played for West Ham and QPR. Unlike Scoular, Frank very much stayed in the background and let Jimmy take the training sessions. Jimmy was an excellent coach and we were delighted to discover that he liked to do a lot of ball work in training, rather than lung-bursting runs. The players took to Jimmy's calm, methodical approach and really enjoyed his sessions.

Adjusting to a new management team is often difficult and it certainly was in this case. In terms of his style and personality Frank was the complete opposite to Jimmy Scoular. He was far more relaxed, and quieter, and we only really had contact with him on match days, and even then it was minimal. On the odd occasion when Frank did come out onto the training field he would wear a tracksuit over his suit, which the players found a bit weird. Some questioned what was he actually doing to earn his salary.

However, results initially picked up after Frank and Jimmy arrived, and we slowly dragged ourselves up the table. In Frank's second game in charge we managed to win our first away game for almost two years, beating Leyton Orient by the odd goal in three at Brisbane Road. It was great to get that monkey off our backs as no matter what we did we couldn't get an away win for neither love nor money during that period. It is strange, because at the end of the day, home or away, football is still eleven versus eleven, but confidence can be a twelfth man, and after we lost a few games away, we developed a mental block that saw us struggle on the road.

With things looking up David Goldstone made some money available for Frank to sign new players. Arriving at the club were Willie Carlin, from Notts County, and winger John Farrington, who came for a record fee of £62,500. I think Willie had played for Frank at his previous club, Leicester, and he was a very experienced pro who knew his way around the leagues. He was getting towards the end of his career, but had great leadership qualities, and he made an immediate impact on and off the pitch. John was also a good signing as he brought flair and pace on the left-hand side.

Things were certainly picking up, and our confidence was soaring when we beat FA Cup holders, Sunderland, 4–1. We mauled them that day and John Farrington became an instant fan favourite as he got himself a hat trick. Shortly afterwards we faced Notts County, and despite the team playing well, our young defender, Leighton Phillips, was getting a lot of stick from the crowd. I'm not too sure what it was over, but the supporters obviously weren't overly impressed with his performance. Entering the final minute of the game the score was tied at 0–0 before Leighton improbably popped up with the winner. He was so pumped up that he stuck two fingers up at the crowd, which as you can imagine didn't go down very well. Leighton was only a young lad, and it is never nice getting barracked by your own supporters, so I think he just lost his head and snapped. Everyone, however, was willing to forgive and forget come the final whistle as his goal brought us a much needed two points (three points for a win wasn't introduced until 1981).

On a roll, we then beat Preston 2–0, and the victory was made even sweeter as I scored my first goal for the club. It is something I will never forget. Leighton Phillips clipped a cross into the near post and I managed to get a yard in front of my marker and flick the ball, with my head, into the far corner. I was ecstatic. What really topped it off was that I was a Grangetown boy, scoring at the Grange End, in front of my family and friends. I've still got the photograph of me scoring the goal and from time to time I think of the incredible feeling I got when the ball hit the back of the net. It gives me goose bumps just thinking about it. I hit the town hard that night to celebrate and I must have had a great time because the next day I couldn't remember a thing about it!

As if things couldn't get any better I was then called up to represent Wales at under-23 level, along with Tony Villars and Derek Showers. I knew I had been playing well, but I never expected an international call up. The game was against our much heralded English counterparts at Ashton Gate and we couldn't have been facing much tougher opponents. England had a superb team, which included Kevin Beattie, Terry McDermott, Trevor Francis, Bob Latchford and Steve Perryman. Wales were a good, battling side in those days, but on paper we didn't have the class to match England. On the pitch, however, we forgot all about reputations, gave it our all, and came away with a creditable 0–0 draw. I was pleased with my display and it certainly gave me a taste for international football. A senior call up was a long way off at this point, but I prayed that one day I would get the chance to represent my country at that level.

With everything going so well the wheels suddenly came off back at Cardiff. After losing 5–2 to Birmingham, in the FA Cup, we then crashed 5–0 to Sheffield Wednesday, before getting beat, 3–1, by Millwall, at Ninian Park. Just as we thought we were out of relegation trouble we were now back scrapping for our lives. Sensing the squad still needed strengthening O'Farrell signed a goalkeeper, Ron Healey, and a defender, Clive Charles. Charlo was a cracking lad, a typical cockney who always had something to say, and a lover of banter. We didn't have many black players at Cardiff at the time and after seeing Charlo in the showers I soon learned that it's true what they say about black men being well endowed! Ron was also a good laugh and Charlo and him were a real double act, keeping the rest of us in stitches. They both certainly lifted the dressing room, but results on the pitch were still mixed.

Entering the final stages of the season we came up against league leaders, Middlesbrough, in desperate need of a win. Belying our lowly league position it was us who looked like title contenders that day as we won 3–2, with the goals coming from Reece, Carlin and Vincent. That result gave us a huge boost and a good chance of staying up.

But then, out of nowhere, Frank O'Farrell resigned to take up a job in the Middle East. We were flabbergasted. Here we were in the middle of a relegation scrap, with just a couple of games to go, and our manager leaves us in the lurch. Thankfully, Jimmy Andrews was appointed in his place and as we were used to seeing more of Jimmy than Frank the change didn't affect us that much.

In Jimmy's first game in charge we got a valuable point at Notts County but then proceeded to lose the next game, 2–1, to Nottingham Forest. Forest had Duncan McKenzie in the side and he tore us to shreds. He was so quick and skilful that he was able to turn me inside out and I felt as though I needed a new cartilage. I remember thinking at one point that the key to snuffing him out would be to get tight but as the ball bounced towards him he back-heeled it over my head and left me for dead. I didn't play against many better players than Duncan and I'm just glad I didn't have to face him every week. I am afraid that, eventually, I would have snapped and put him in the infirmary.

Time was beginning to run out in our battle to beat the drop but at least we had two home games to finish off the season. Matters were still in our own hands and if we could win one of those games, or avoid defeat in both, we would be safe. The first game was against Leyton Orient and we managed to scramble a 1–1 draw, with Gil Reece scoring. The upshot was that a draw in our last game against fellow strugglers Crystal Palace would be enough to save us.

As I said earlier, with Malcolm Allison at the helm, Palace had been promotion favourites, but they had struggled badly and only a win against us would save them. It was a huge game for both clubs, but the Cardiff supporters were like a twelfth man, as they came out in their droves to support us in our do-or-die game. With 27,000 crammed into Ninian Park, urging us to victory, we actually went behind before Tony Villars popped up to equalise, which got the old ground rocking. Palace never recovered and we managed to see out the game, and to stay up by a single point. Palace went down and Malcolm certainly wasn't seen puffing his cigar that day!

Saving ourselves in such a dramatic manner was becoming our party trick, but sooner or later our luck was bound to run out. Everyone connected with the club felt that if we went another summer without significant investment the writing would be on the wall. Jimmy Andrews looked to be a very capable trainer, and manager, but he couldn't be expected to get results when he was fighting with one arm tied behind his back.

During the season we again won the Welsh Cup, against that well known Welsh side, Stourbridge. In those days a few English teams were invited to take part in the competition, such as Shrewsbury and Hereford, which always gave it added spice because you never wanted to see an English team win *your* cup. Once again we had European football to look forward to but everyone's minds were preoccupied with what promised to be another long hard slog in the league, unless a miracle happened.

# 7

## Rock Bottom

During the previous two years my life had changed beyond all recognition. I had become an established first-team player, had got married and moved into a home of my own. Yet there was more to come. Early in 1974 Ann announced that she was pregnant. She gave birth to our son, Darren, on 10 September and everything changed from that moment onwards. I was no longer playing just for myself; I now had a wife and child to support. Being a father was wonderful, but it was also a daunting responsibility for someone about to turn twenty-one. Football could not be considered a hobby; it was a career that put food on the table and a roof over our heads.

Going into pre-season I really had the bit between my teeth. Whilst I had played in virtually every game since my debut I was determined to cement my place. Everything Jimmy asked of me I did in double-quick time. There was no way I could afford to start slacking.

I don't suppose anyone expected us to be big spenders that summer, but I hoped that a little money would be available for one or two quality additions. Chairman David Goldstone, however, informed Jimmy Andrews that if he wanted new recruits he would have to sell before he could buy. I felt sorry for Jimmy, but I also had sympathy for Mr Goldstone's position. It was clear that the club was in a bit of a mess and that we were struggling financially. However, instead of getting caught up with the politics, as some players tended to, I got my head down and trained as hard as possible. As long as I prepared properly I couldn't do any more. Besides, I was paid to play football, not to fight battles in the boardroom.

Following David Goldstone's bombshell Jimmy had no option but to let go of some of our high earners, guys like Andy McCulloch, Bobby Woodruff and Gary Bell. I was gutted to see those three leave, as not only were they cracking players, but also they were close pals. Belly had of course been my best man at my wedding, and we used to knock about with each other a lot. I had also spent a lot of time with Andy, as he had digs down in Grangetown, and Woody was someone whose company I always enjoyed.

With no new signings materialising before the start of the season it was no surprise that we had an appalling start. In fact we only managed to pick up four points from our first ten fixtures and in that spell we also lost four consecutive home games. Quite astonishingly, one of those games was against Tommy Docherty's Manchester United, who had been relegated the previous season, less than ten years after becoming champions of Europe. Over the years I have been told that there was appalling violence during the game, with both sets of supporters throwing concrete blocks and darts at each other. Even after the game it seems there was a full-scale riot outside Cardiff Central station. But it's amazing: while I can remember the game, I can't recall any trouble. I was probably so immersed in trying to keep Lou Macari, Steve Coppell and Sammy McIlroy quiet that I failed to notice the carnage around me.

Stuck in a deep rut the atmosphere around Ninian Park started to get a little fraught. It was obvious we needed a boost from somewhere; otherwise we were in for a long, hard, morale-sapping season. But the poor results continued and crowds began to dwindle, which of course didn't help the finances. As for those supporters who did show up, they were on the war path, letting us know in no uncertain terms that what we were providing wasn't their idea of entertainment.

The fans had every right to be upset. They paid their money and were entitled to their opinion, but the little confidence that we did have began to drain away. Some of the lads were very sensitive to the crowd shouting at them and it really affected how they played. If the crowd had a pop at me it was water off a duck's back. I was so caught up in the game that I hardly heard a thing, but not everyone was able to do that.

The stress began to show on even the most mild-mannered member of staff. In an away game, to York City, our gentle, churchgoing physio, Ron Durham, snapped. I think the York fans were giving us stick and for some reason Ron threw a bucket of water over them, which almost started a riot. It was totally out of character and shows the pressure we all felt, but it certainly gave us a good laugh on the journey home.

Things weren't much better in the European Cup Winners Cup against the Hungarian outfit, Ferencvaros, who beat us 2–0 at Ninian Park. For the away leg I remember that the Ferencvaros board arranged for us to have a meal the night before the game. It turned out that the restaurant was part of a nightclub and to this day I am convinced it was a deliberate ploy to put temptation in our path. Jimmy Andrews immediately saw the danger, and watched us like hawks, before shepherding us back to our rooms, thus ensuring that we weren't tempted by the booze and the ladies. To be fair it probably wouldn't have done us any harm if we had stayed out all night as we ended up losing the game 4–1.

Jimmy tried his best to wheel and deal in the transfer market, but he still had to sell more players before he could bring anyone in. Leighton Phillips was subsequently transferred to Aston Villa for £80,000, which was a great move for him, and a good deal for the club, but he was another quality player we were going to miss. Our record signing, John Farrington, who had only joined the previous year, was then exchanged for John Buchanan of Northampton Town. In our predicament we needed a bit more grit, and although it was frustrating to lose another good player, Buchanan was just what we needed at that point.

Buchy was a fiery Scotsman, a guy who worked his nuts off for ninety minutes. He also got more than his fair share of goals from midfield and more often than not they were screamers. In addition he was good around the dressing room, being as mad as the proverbial hatter. At Cardiff the Welsh boys always had a bit of banter with the Scots but if the English lads waded in we would join forces and put them in their place. It was never nasty stuff, just good-natured ribbing, and Buchy loved nothing more than questioning the English contingent's parentage.

By this stage Ann and I had managed to buy a house in Llanedeyrn and as luck would have it Buchy moved in across the road from us. As we lived so close we usually ended up giving each other lifts to training and to matches. Then, on Sundays, Buchy would join me and my father-in-law, Frank, for a few pints at the Pennsylvania pub. He was a good laugh and he soon became one of the Pennsylvania's favourite patrons.

Though Buchy added some grit to the side, we were still low on numbers, and I was shocked when Jimmy decided to let Don Murray leave. Don had become part of the furniture at Cardiff City; he had been one of our key players on and off the pitch for years and his advice had been invaluable to me as a young lad breaking into the team. I think Jimmy may have felt that Don wasn't getting any younger, and he certainly wasn't as mobile as he used to be, but I still felt he could do a good job. The thought of playing without Don by my side terrified me.

However, after Buchy came into the team, and with Don gone, results picked up and although we were drawing far too many games we at least stopped losing. In consecutive games I managed to score against Forest and Orient and we also surprisingly beat some of the big guns in the division, the likes of Sunderland, Villa and Norwich. From looking down and out we went on a run that saw us lose just once in twelve games.

At the turn of the New Year I was thrilled to find that we had been drawn to play my heroes, Leeds United, at Elland Road, in the FA Cup. I had to pinch myself that I was going to be on the same pitch as the likes of Billy Bremner, Norman Hunter and Allan Clarke. Things got even better when I was named as captain, a real dream come true. I remember as I walked towards the centre circle for the coin toss that I couldn't believe that I was about to shake hands with my idol, Billy Bremner. I had once pretended to be Billy on the streets of Grangetown and now here I was, ready to do battle with him. I had pictured this moment in my dreams but unfortunately things didn't go to plan. As I shook hands with my hero he patted me patronisingly on the back of my head and said, 'All the best, sonny.'

'All the best, sonny?' I was furious.

It was obvious that it was a mind game, designed to make me feel inferior. And it worked, because it left me steaming. I spent the whole game trying to kick Bremner as hard as I could but I couldn't get near him. He would keep the ball for a maximum of two touches before releasing it to a teammate. It was amazing to watch how the entire game seemed to pass through him. He was such a dominant personality on the pitch. Predictably, Leeds strolled to a 4–1 win and while I was not best pleased with Billy's wind-up antics I felt privileged to be on the same pitch as him.

Just as we started to move away from the relegation zone we got murdered 5–1 at Millwall. Matters weren't helped when I was attacked by a fan. Feeling humiliated at the score-line, I got frustrated and when their keeper, Ray Goddard, came to collect a cross I 'accidentally' collided with him. Crashing hard to the ground Ray let out a cry and I thought, 'Shit, I better pretend I'm hurt to so I don't get sent off.' As I lay on the ground I crawled up into a ball, holding my head and making some moaning sounds, hoping it would earn me sympathy from the ref. As Ron Durham tended to me I had a quick peek and saw that Ray was being stretchered off the field with an oxygen mask over his face.

'Shit, I've killed him,' I thought.

Seeing Ray in such bad shape made me stay down a bit longer, pretending that he was the one who had hurt me. I was, however, convinced that I was going to get sent off. Finally, getting to my feet I was oblivious to the trouble that my antics had caused in the stands. Looking around, the place was like a war zone, with the two sets of fans getting stuck into each other. Distracted by the carnage I didn't notice a crazed Millwall fan come running towards me. Then, at the last moment, just as he swung at me, I saw him out of the corner of my eye. Ducking and weaving, in a manoeuvre that Muhammed Ali would have been proud of, I got the little toe rag in a head lock. As I squeezed his neck, determined to strangle him, the police stepped in and carted him off. After all the drama I had completely forgotten about the possibility of being dismissed, but, incredibly, so had the referee, and the game continued without me even getting a talking-to.

After the game, as we were licking our wounds in the changing room, there was a knock on the door and two police officers marched in. My heart was in my mouth. I was sure they were going to arrest me for murdering Ray! Luckily, Ray had survived my 'attack' and was laid up in hospital with concussion. It turned out that the police only wanted to know if I was going to press charges against the fan. In no uncertain terms I told them, 'You must be joking. If I ever played here again I'd get lynched!'

That game marked the beginning of the end for us. Our form nosedived. In the last seventeen games of the season we only won twice and found ourselves rooted in the relegation zone. Morale was rock bottom and we were all very frustrated. In a home game, against Sheffield Wednesday, I remember George Smith being substituted and as he walked off the pitch he threw his shirt at Jimmy Andrews. Unsurprisingly, George didn't play much after that and he was swiftly moved on in the summer.

Unlike previous seasons there was to be no great escape. This time we were relegated before our final game against Bolton, which we also happened to lose. The warning signs had been there for years and matters hadn't been helped by not bringing in adequate replacements after some of our experienced guys left during the campaign.

Things just seemed to go from bad to worse, even in the Welsh Cup, which we had dominated in recent years. In the final we were humiliated by Wrexham, who beat us 5–2 on aggregate. That was rock bottom; we couldn't do anything right. In the end we were desperate for the season to be over and desperately hoped that in the summer Mr Goldstone would somehow find some money to let Jimmy sign new players. If we didn't then I really feared for our future.

# 8

# On the Up

It had been obvious for some time that while David Goldstone was doing a tremendous job balancing the books we desperately needed new investment if we were going to move forward. We had lost too many quality players over the last few years and the warning signs had been apparent for quite a while. If we again failed to spend I felt that we would go into a terminal decline. But our prayers were finally answered in the summer of 1975, when a local consortium completed a takeover and promised to invest in the squad. The consortium was put together by local businessman Clive Griffiths and he was joined by politician and hotelier, Stefan Terleski, as well as Tony Clemo, Eddie Jones, Hyman 'Tiny' Latner and two businessmen from the north-east of England, Bob Grogan and Jack Leonard.

Stefan was elected club chairman, but it seemed that Bob and Jack were the real money men. They owned a company called the Kenton Utilities Group and had been very successful in the business world. Although they continued to live in the north-east, and were mad Newcastle United fans, they travelled down to Cardiff, via a private jet, almost every week. They were incredibly enthusiastic and the players took to them straightaway. It helped that they were always happy to have a chat and took a real interest in all of us. They also remained very down to earth, and could join in the dressing-room banter, which was rare for directors.

With new investment coming into the club, Jimmy Andrews decided to clear the decks and bring in some new faces. It was of no surprise that George Smith, after the shirt-throwing incident the previous season, was the first to leave; he was sold to Swansea. A whole raft of other players also went through the exit door, such as John Impey, Johnny Vincent, Jimmy McInch, Jack Whitham and Dave Powell. Some of them dropped down to play non-league while Dave Powell enlisted in the police force. It was especially sad to see my old youth teammates, Messrs McInch and Impey, depart. I was now one of the few remaining from that tremendous FA Youth Cup team.

Making a surprise return to the club that summer was the conqueror of Real Madrid, Brian Clark, who came in on a free transfer from Millwall. It was great to see an old face and have him around the place again. Clarkey always gave 100 per cent and despite the fact that he was nearing the end of his career, and didn't score as regularly as he once had, he was a true professional and set an example to the younger players.

Another great addition to the team was Tony Evans, who we also managed to sign on a free transfer. Evo turned out to be a great goalscorer over the next couple of years and what immediately struck me about him was his pace. He was greased lightning. I hated facing him in training games because when he came at you full pelt he could leave you for dead. While Evo was a great lad we soon learned that we needed two mirrors in the changing room, one for him and another for the rest of us. Despite the fact that he looked like a porn star – with his handlebar moustache and bouffant hair – he really fancied himself as a ladies' man. To be fair to him he always seemed to do all right for himself and I remember he even had some groupies, who followed him home and away.

Everyone was pleased with the additions of Evo and Clarkey but Jimmy's next signing really got the club buzzing. He somehow managed to pull off a sensational coup when he signed Wales international, Mike England, from the Seattle Sounders. Mike had enjoyed a tremendous career in England with Spurs, where he had won the FA Cup and the League Cup as well as the UEFA Cup. In his heyday he was regarded as one of the top defenders in Britain, and, because he was Welsh, he was a real icon in Cardiff.

I was thrilled to have Mike at the club because I knew I could learn so much from him. Over the years he had been one of my favourite players and the chance to train and play alongside someone of his calibre was a real thrill. From the start Mike had a huge impact on and off the pitch and he was brilliant at passing on tips to help improve my game. We used to spend hours after training together and he would show me the correct technique to head a ball when clearing it. Someone would pump a ball into the penalty area and Mike would leap impossibly high, strain his neck backwards, before then snapping his head forward to meet the ball with an almighty thump, a technique that would see it travel halfway up the pitch. I watched him in awe. After weeks of practice my heading significantly improved but I could never head the ball as far as Mike. It was as if his forehead was a trampoline.

The next lesson Mike taught me was on how to deal with crosses: when one is delivered into the box, it is advisable to head the ball back in the direction from whence it came. That way you know exactly where everyone is and you are not putting the ball into unknown territory. In defensive terms, the team is also already set up to cope with another cross from that direction. It all seems so simple, but throughout his time at Cardiff Mike was a goldmine of information and he helped me become a better player.

When the season got underway our results were mixed. We lost to the likes of Grimsby and Palace, but we beat Brighton and drew with Bury. It was hardly surprising that our form was erratic, as not only were we blooding our new signings, but we were also adjusting to life in the third division. The third tier was very physical, which surprised some of the boys, and we learned that we would have to scrap and earn the right to play. It was, however, a lot slower than the second division, which suited me down to the ground!

A few games into the season Jimmy made another shrewd signing when he brought Doug Livermore to the club from Norwich City. Doug had come through the ranks at Liverpool, under Bill Shankly, and had then joined Norwich, where he had been part of a promotion-winning side. He provided a touch of class in the middle of the field and over the course of the season he was a real asset in opening up defences. Off the field he was a typical Scouser, always winding everyone up, and in the middle of any mischief. He and Tony Evans became great mates and he fitted in seamlessly.

Doug was the missing piece in Jimmy's jigsaw and once he arrived we felt like a team and started to put some results together. In one of those games, a 4–1 victory over Mansfield, I got my first goal of the season but I have always remembered the game for another reason – our kit. Bizarrely, we had to wear Mansfield's yellow away strip because when we arrived we found our home kit clashed with theirs and we hadn't brought a spare set of jerseys with us. After the game we asked if we could wear their kit every week!

With the team finding its form Willie Anderson returned from his summer stint in the USA and played as if he had never been away. We knew that Willie could beat a man, and whip in a great cross, and our forwards loved having him on the field, as he provided such fantastic service for them. Jimmy continued to tinker with our formation and one of his concerns was that we didn't have enough height in the middle of the park. As a result he played me in midfield. He told me that my job would be not only to shield our back four, but also to pop up with late runs into the box and get on the end of Willie's crosses. I hadn't played much football in midfield but I relished the opportunity to get on the ball more and to prove that I wasn't just a brawler.

One of my first games in the new role came against Wrexham at Ninian Park and it went better than anyone could have anticipated. Amazingly, I scored two goals and in the final minute of the game I was even given the opportunity to complete a hat trick. Following a trip on Willie Anderson we were awarded a penalty, and, although I wasn't the designated taker, I stepped forward to take the kick. We were already 3–0 up and I was on such a high that I felt certain I would score. Strolling up to the spot I decided against smashing the ball and instead tried to side foot it into the corner. To my horror, the keeper correctly guessed which way I was going to put it, and parried the ball round the post. I was gutted. My chance to score a hat trick at Ninian Park was gone but despite the miss I couldn't fail but to be happy with my afternoon's work. Walking into the changing room I was expecting a pat on the back from Jimmy Andrews but instead he lambasted me for taking the penalty. He even said that if we missed out on promotion due to goal difference, I would be to blame. The wind was swiftly and unceremoniously taken out of my sails.

By this stage we were finally clicking as a team and the signing of Australia World Cup star, Adrian Alston, from Luton Town, was the catalyst that made us promotion contenders. Adrian was probably the most skilful player I had ever seen and he did things with a ball that I didn't think were possible. He strode into our dressing room with a broad grin and a cocky, loud demeanour that demanded our attention. We instantly took to him. All day long he played pranks to keep us entertained. His favourite was to wait until one of the lads jumped in the shower, which gave him the chance to rub deep heat into their underwear. Watching the unfortunate victim hopping around and swearing bloody murder was always great value. I never tired of it, although maybe that's because Adrian never picked on me.

Adrian instantly became the darling of our supporters when he scored two goals on his debut against Chesterfield and in the process struck up a great understanding with Evo. It was immediately apparent that the two of them, sparking off each other, were going to cause opposition defences all sorts of problems. If you took your eye off one of them for a second the next thing you knew the ball would be in the back of the net.

I was really excited about the prospects for the team. Strong at the back, and electric going forward, with a nice mix of youth and experience, it was the perfect recipe for success. The standard of our football was out of this world at times but we could also fight as well, so no matter who we faced, we could always hold our own. Our dressing room was bubbling too. It was full of larger-than-life personalities, who lit up a room, and when I think back to those times I do so with fond memories. Without a doubt this was one of my happiest periods as a professional footballer.

Everything was going so well but it almost ended in disaster for me during a game at Gillingham. Their keeper punted the ball downfield, and, as I went to meet it with my head, a Gillingham player proceeded to knee me in the face. The blow knocked me out cold and the next thing I remember is waking up in an ambulance on the side of the pitch, where I was told that I had swallowed my tongue and stopped breathing. I don't know if this is true but I've been told that our physio, Ron Durham, had to use the corner flag to prise my tongue out of my throat before giving me the kiss of life. I know I have a big mouth, but I don't think it's big enough for a corner flag! Once Ron had worked his magic I was fine, but my wife, Ann, was at home and feared the worst. She had been watching *Grandstand* with her parents, and a newsflash had popped up saying that I had been seriously injured. At one point the reporter even suggested that because I was seen receiving mouth-to-mouth resuscitation I may have died. Understandably, Ann was worried sick and frantically tried to get in touch with the club, but this was before the days of mobile phones so she couldn't reach anyone. Finally, one of the club directors contacted her to assure her that I was okay and would be kept in hospital overnight as a precaution. She tells me that she was terribly upset but when I finally got home I found my life-insurance policy spread out on the floor and her bags packed!

Despite this brush with death I recovered so quickly that I was back in action for our next home game against Colchester United. Although I was a little apprehensive, once I got the first header out of the way I forgot all about the drama of the previous week and went about my business as usual. Once again we put in another encouraging performance and goals from Evo and Adrian gave us a 2–0 win, which put us in the top two.

Going into the Xmas period we seemed to be cruising, but then we got a rude awakening on Boxing Day when we lost 4–0 at Swindon. We were never in the game and it certainly looked as though a few of us had enjoyed a bit too much turkey the day before. On the journey back to Cardiff, the mood was sombre. Luckily, we had the chance to get the defeat out of our system the next day when we faced Peterborough at Ninian Park. It's funny. You never see teams play two matches on consecutive days in the modern era, but when I played it seemed to happen all the time. The players of today moan if they play too often but I would have happily had a game every day. After all, the more you play the less you train and I know which I prefer. If I earned the money the current generation of professional footballers do then I would play two games a day, no problem. Even now!

Against Peterborough we came out all guns blazing. Our pride had been hurt and I remember Mike England really got us going in the changing room beforehand. It was imperative that we proved to the fans, and to ourselves, that the Swindon result was a blip. In truth Peterborough didn't have a chance as we played them off the park to win 5–2. Evo added another two goals to his tally for the season, as did I. I was by now really enjoying playing in midfield. I would win the ball and give it to our match winners – Doug, Willie, Evo or Adrian – as swiftly as possible and make a nuisance of myself at set pieces. It wasn't always pretty, but it was very effective.

In January we came up against fellow promotion chasers, Brighton and Hove Albion, and the game was shown live on *Match of the Day*. Whenever the cameras came to town the posers in the team, such as Evo, always made sure they had their hair cut and their moustache clipped to perfection. Adrian Alston was another who loved the cameras and he almost made a name for himself when, straight from kickoff, he spotted the keeper off his line and tried his luck. Everything seemed to happen in slow motion, and for a moment it looked as if he had done it, but the ball agonisingly missed the top corner by a matter of inches. That was the sort of player Adrian was; he could do outrageous things off the cuff and if I had been a fan I would happily have paid to watch him play.

Unfortunately, we lost 1–0 to Brighton and then shortly thereafter we were taken apart by league leaders Hereford, who beat us 4–1. Hereford were a strong side, with the likes of former England international Terry Paine playing for them, but it was still a shock to find ourselves outfought and, at times, outclassed. It was an experience that definitely knocked our confidence.

Away to Walsall, in our next game, we struggled to get the Hereford aberration out of our systems and were lacklustre in the first half. At the break we were 2–0 down and feeling sorry for ourselves. Jimmy banged our heads together at half-time and knocked us into shape. He told us that it was moments like these that would define our season and if we wanted to be serious promotion contenders we had to go out in the second half and fight for every ball, and try to salvage the game. Feeling reinvigorated we went out with a renewed sense of urgency and our second-half performance was a dramatic improvement. Adrian scored two goals to draw us level and then late in the game I got my head on the end of a Willie Anderson cross to score a dramatic winner. We went absolutely mental and ran over to celebrate with our little mob of fans, who were bouncing around as if they were on pogo sticks. At that moment I knew that we had what it took to get promoted.

With the business end of the season approaching Scottish mid-fielder, Alan Campbell, who we all called 'AC', joined the club from Birmingham. AC was a lovely player. He could spray the ball all over the field and he always managed to find a yard of space. Going into the home stretch he really settled us down and if you were in trouble you knew you could give the ball to AC and he would conjure something out of nothing.

In fact after AC came into the team we only conceded one goal in our last nine games. Our defence was so tight we knew that if we scored we would win the game because with Adrian and Evo around we were always guaranteed goals. Everyone was working hard for each other and determined to get promoted at the first time of asking. The last thing we wanted was another season in the third division.

In one of our last remaining games we faced Malcolm Allison's Crystal Palace at Selhurst Park. We won 1–0 but, in all honesty, it was a massacre. It was one of the most one-sided games I can remember. Malcolm was obviously sore afterwards, as he tried to portray Cardiff as a little club, getting above our station. He famously bet that we wouldn't attract more than twenty thousand fans to Ninian Park for our top-of-the-table clash with Hereford the following week. If we exceeded twenty thousand he said he would send us a crate of champagne. His comments really wound us up. I was always confident that the fans would come out in force for the Hereford game but even I was surprised when a huge crowd of 36,000 turned up. Spurred on by Allison's comments the atmosphere was phenomenal and we fed off the energy of the packed stadium by winning 2–0, and avenged our humiliation from earlier in the season. Doug Livermore and AC got the goals and I remember that the Grange End was as high as a kite. We never did see that crate of champagne from Malcolm either!

After that result we knew that barring disaster we were as good as up. However, we certainly made hard work of it as we drew our next two games and that meant that we had to beat Bury away, in the final game, to be sure of promotion. Once more our fans turned out in their numbers to support us and the game felt like we were at home as the Cardiff fans outnumbered, and out-sang, the Bury supporters. Their marvellous backing eased our nerves and I managed to set up the vital goal when I flicked on the ball for Adrian to rifle home. When the final whistle blew our supporters were delirious, invading the field and carrying us on their shoulders. What a feeling!

Trying to get back to the changing room, after celebrating with the fans, was a nightmare. Everyone was pulling at my strip and hair and slapping me on the back. The only way I could get through the melee was to crawl on my hands and knees. When I finally arrived in the changing room I found the promotion party in full swing and the place jam-packed with players, management and directors, every one of them singing and dancing. Bottles of champagne were popping everywhere and I was drunk before I even left the ground. We stayed in Manchester that night and Bob Grogan took us all to a fancy restaurant. He told us that we could eat and drink whatever we liked. The lads took full advantage of Bob's kind offer and got plastered again. It was a memorable night and a special occasion.

Not only had we enjoyed a successful season in the league, but we had also gone on a good run in the FA Cup. In the first round we had humiliated Exeter 6–2, with Adrian getting a hat trick. We then beat Wycombe, and Orient, before getting knocked out by Southend in controversial circumstances. The score was tied at 1–1, but with the last kick of the game they scored the winner via a blatant handball. We were all incensed but the referee waved away our protests and that was that.

We enjoyed a bit more luck in the Welsh Cup, especially against our fierce rivals Swansea City in the semi-finals. At Ninian Park we drew 1–1 and looked to have a mountain to climb in the return game at the Vetch. The Vetch was a grim place to go for any team, not just Cardiff. It was a ramshackle little ground, in which the fans seemed to breathe down your neck. Some players were intimidated before they had even set foot in the place but I was in my element. The more the crowd baited me the better I played and I loved giving the Cardiff fans something to cheer about. This would usually come courtesy of one of my trademark tackles.

Some people are amazed at just how strong the hatred is between Cardiff and Swansea but the derby game is the be all and end all for both sets of supporters. I don't quite know where the animosity comes from but they truly despise each other. It is strange because in my day the players at the two clubs got on very well and on occasion we would even socialise together. To this day I am still good mates with Alan Curtis. However, you could never let the fans know that you were friendly with the opposition, they just wouldn't understand. To Cardiff fans Swansea are the enemy and all your efforts must be channelled into not only defeating them, but also embarrassing them. It's amazing. I played for Cardiff over twenty-five years ago, but to this day Swansea fans don't forget. A few years ago I was in Swansea and as I crossed the road someone shouted from a passing van, 'Oi Dwyer, fuck off back to Cardiff.' Unbelievable!

Thankfully, in the second leg we really delivered the result our fans craved as we beat the Jacks 3–0. They were delirious as we celebrated in the home of our rivals. It was a sweet victory.

Once again we reached the Welsh Cup final where we came up against our foes from the league that year, Hereford United. In another enthralling encounter we drew 3–3 at Edgar Street, where I managed to get two goals to take my tally to ten for the season. The second leg, at Ninian Park, was played in atrocious conditions and as such we couldn't get our passing game going. Fighting against the elements we lost the game 3–2 but despite losing to our English rivals we would again participate in the European Cup Winners Cup the next season as the Welsh FA refused to put English winners forward.

All in all it had been a fantastic season; full of laughter, memorable performances and some brilliant results. We were on a high and looking forward to being back in the second division. I had no doubt that the team would do very well, if we could just stay together and bring in a few reinforcements. Wishful thinking indeed!

# 9

# New Division, Same Old Story

Having enjoyed such a successful campaign the team were really looking forward to testing ourselves in a division in which we had been nothing more than relegation fodder in years gone by. Jimmy Andrews had performed a minor miracle in turning the team around and I was confident that we would not only be able to hold our own, but could also be dark horses for promotion.

Our prospects, however, were dented when Mike England departed. I think he had been looking for a managerial role and was disappointed that the club wouldn't consider him, probably because of the excellent job Jimmy Andrews was doing. Jimmy was also no doubt a little apprehensive at having a man of Mike's stature hanging around in the background, waiting to take his job, so it was no surprise that player and club agreed to a parting of the ways. It was sad to see Mike leave as he had been a huge part in not only the team's success, but also in my own.

Local boys, Tony Villars and Gil Reece, as well as old stalwart Brian Clark, also left but we managed to bring in some fresh faces, with Peter Jackson signing from Leicester and Alan Sealey joining the coaching staff from West Ham. Alan fitted in instantly. He was outspoken, brash and a wind-up merchant, just like the rest of us. Not only did the players all take to him as a person, but he was also a fantastic coach, who made his sessions interesting and enjoyable.

With things shaping up nicely I did something really stupid, which I haven't told many people about until now. I mentioned earlier in the book that I had enjoyed playing baseball as a teenager, but even when I became a professional footballer I continued to play for Grange Catholics during the summer. No one at Ninian Park knew about it, as I was sure they would have stopped me, but I saw it as a good way to keep fit and stay in touch with the boys I had grown up with.

Just as the baseball season was coming to a close Cardiff were drawn to play the Swiss side, Servette, in the first round of the European Cup Winners Cup on 4 August 1976. Two days before the match I had an important baseball game, which I was very reluctant to miss. I reasoned that baseball is hardly the most taxing, or physical, of sports, so it wouldn't be a problem if I played. Disaster struck, however, when I rounded the bases; my ankle suddenly crumpled underneath me and caused me to limp away in agony.

When I woke up the next morning my ankle was the size of a balloon and I couldn't walk. I knew I couldn't tell Jimmy that I had done it playing baseball, as he would have killed me, so I told him that I had fallen down the stairs. On seeing the state of my ankle Jimmy sent me to the hospital where an X-ray subsequently revealed that I had broken my ankle and that I would have to spend the next six weeks in plaster. That meant I would have to sit out the first few games of the season as well as our games in Europe. Missing the start of the season was a hammer blow and I realised that now I was a professional footballer my baseball days had to come to an end, sad though that prospect was.

What really brought home my stupidity was that Ann had given birth to our second child that summer, a beautiful little girl we named Claire. Not only was I being irresponsible with my career by playing baseball but also Ann was faced with the prospect of looking after a baby, as well as her grumpy husband, who was on crutches. I certainly wasn't the most popular man in Cardiff at this time I can tell you.

Though the lads started the season brightly, by winning 2–0 at Charlton, the team then went on a poor run, which saw us win only one more time before I finally returned to face Millwall at the end of September. It was great to be back and despite being a little rusty I put in a decent display, at full back, as we drew 0–0.

Without getting much chance to catch my breath the team then had a big European game on the horizon, against Dinamo Tbilisi, a team from Georgia, which, in those far-off days of communist rule was part of the Soviet Union. In my absence the lads had beaten Servette over two legs and had then beaten the Georgians, 1–0, at Ninian Park. I was fit for the second leg against Dinamo and was looking forward to playing in their huge stadium, which could hold over one hundred thousand people.

We flew to Moscow a few days before the game and spent some time taking in sights such as the Kremlin and Red Square. Thanks to the dead hand of communism, poverty was rife. The Russians we came across were downtrodden, with little reason to smile, and it broke my heart to see people eking out an existence. Our hotel must once have been very glamorous, with its marble floors and granite walls, but it had long since seen better days as the paint was peeling off the walls and the springs in the beds were poking out. The food was also horrific. All they seemed to serve were hardboiled eggs and stale meat.

We arrived in Tbilisi the day before the game and found it completely different. The Georgian people were more upbeat, probably because they were slightly more prosperous than those in Moscow, and there wasn't the same intimidating atmosphere where you felt you had to watch what you said and where you went.

Tbilisi's fans certainly turned out in their numbers for the match and filled the 100,000-seater stadium with thousands more locked out. I didn't realise that Cardiff City were such a big draw in Georgia! I had never seen anything like it; people balanced precariously wherever they could in order to see the game. Though we went into the encounter with a 1–0 lead we knew that we would have to perform to our full potential to beat them in their own backyard, particularly in the face of such hostile fans. For whatever reason they hated us and it was certainly more intimidating playing a game behind the Iron Curtain, in front of thousands of nutters, than it was at the Vetch or the Den. We found it hard to concentrate, probably because we feared we would get lynched if we started playing well, and partly because we were all starving after boycotting the hotel food. Unsurprisingly, we lost 3–0. There was, however, no shame in losing to them as they were a great team. I think they even beat Liverpool in Europe that year, but we were all glad to get out of there in one piece.

Being out of Europe we could now concentrate on the league, in which we had suffered from an indifferent start. Maybe we became a little too cocky, after our success the previous season, because we started conceding some comical goals. Jimmy decided that we needed to shore up the back four so he went out and purchased Paul Went from Portsmouth. Wenty was a humongous bloke, with long blonde hair down to his shoulders, and despite having hair like a girl he gave us a bit of steel with his no-nonsense approach.

Although Wenty was brought in to help prevent goals the poor bloke had a shocking first few games. On his debut, against Bolton, he conceded a penalty but thankfully we went on to win the game 3–2. Then in his next game, against Plymouth, he gave away another penalty, but Evo and I got him out of jail with a goal apiece, which saw us win the game 2–1. We gave him some good-natured banter, which he took in his stride, and he soon became a very effective member of the side.

Just as we had started to string some results together our star player, Adrian Alston, left to join Tampa Bay Rowdies in the USA. Adrian was a showman and I could see why playing in America was such a big attraction to him. America was the place to be in those days, as that was where many of the game's biggest stars – the likes of Pele, Best, Moore and Beckenbauer – plied their trade. No doubt he was also looking forward to the sun and beaches of Florida rather than the cold, wet and windy winter days at Ninian Park. I loved playing at Ninian Park, in all conditions, but I did sometimes think of the great lifestyle on offer Stateside. Unfortunately, I don't think there was a lot of call in America for a lad from Grangetown to kick people!

Jimmy signed Steve Grapes from Norwich to replace Adrian and although Steve was a great lad, and a decent player, it didn't work out for him at Cardiff. As a result we were not only conceding too many goals but also we weren't scoring as many. Slowly but surely we sank down the table. By Christmas we were firmly rooted in the bottom half and matters were made much worse when we had a nightmare at Carlisle. Peter 'Leo' Sayer, Buchy and Evo put us into a 3–1 lead and with just seven minutes remaining we were in cruise control. Completely dominating the play there looked to be no danger of us not picking up anything less than two points, a celebratory crate of beer, as well as fish and chips, for the journey home. However, the final minutes of the game resulted in the most remarkable sequence of events I have ever witnessed on a football field.

Carlisle managed to grab a fortuitous consolation goal, but rather than just see the game out we completely lost our heads. Straight from kickoff they won the ball back and scored the equaliser. We were shell shocked. Just a minute earlier we had been two goals in front, but in a flash it was all square. At this stage we needed someone to put his foot on the ball and calm us down, to make sure that we at least left with a point. Unfortunately, however, all common sense went out of the window. Deep panic set in and in the dying moments Carlisle scored the winner. For over eighty minutes we had played very well, but then threw all of our hard work away and somehow contrived to lose 4–3.

Before we had even started to walk down the tunnel I could hear Jimmy blowing his top. He was red in the face and every word that came out of his mouth was followed by spit. The trip back to Cardiff from Carlisle is never that comfortable but it is made especially awkward when the manager won't even let you speak. For six hours I rattled my brain to think of things I could have done better but it really was hard to take that for eighty-three minutes we had them in our pocket and had then managed to lose the game.

The problem was that we were missing Adrian's flair and his ability to fashion something out of nothing. Action was urgently needed and Jimmy Andrews responded to the crisis by making the biggest managerial gamble of his life: the signing of the mercurial Robin Friday from Reading. Robin had acquired quite a reputation in the game, not only for being one of the best talents outside of the top flight, but also for his intolerant attitude towards players, managers and officials. When I heard that we had signed him I was intrigued as there was no doubt that as a player he could improve us.

But would he fit into the dressing room?

Before I even had a chance to meet him I feared the worst. On the day he was due to arrive in Cardiff we were training at Ninian Park when Harry Parsons got a phone call from the police. He was told that Robin Friday was being held at Cardiff Central station as he had travelled down from Reading with a platform-only ticket. Robin claimed that City would pay his rail fare so Harry had no choice but to go to the station, pay the fare and bring our rebellious new recruit to Ninian Park to sign his contract.

Matters got even worse when, shortly thereafter, Harry took Robin to look at a bungalow for rent in St Athan. While they were in the house Robin decided to nick the silverware! After the owner of the house called the club, and threatened to take them to court, a very embarrassed Harry got the objects back from Robin, drove back to the house and apologised profusely to the outraged owner.

At this stage I still hadn't met Robin, but the stories were doing the rounds among the lads. When he showed up for training I noticed that he had the words 'Mild' and 'Bitter' tattooed under his nipples. I thought to myself, 'Bloody hell, who is this bloke?' I remember he used to wear the same jeans, T-shirt and denim jacket every day and would carry all his worldly goods around in a plastic carrier bag. He was like a gypsy. When we travelled back from away games he would nearly always ask the coach driver to stop in the middle of nowhere. We could be anywhere, in the countryside, the motorway, on a roundabout, in all sorts of weather, but he would just get out and walk. God knows where he went.

After speaking to Robin it was clear that something wasn't quite right. He always seemed to have a mad glare in his eye and sometimes he would be so hyper he would be bouncing off the walls. It didn't take much to set him off and he thought nothing of smacking someone in the face if he didn't like what they had said. In one training session I threw the ball to one of the lads and it accidentally hit Robin in the face. Steve Grapes laughed, which enraged Robin, who promptly knocked him out. Poor Steve was in a neck brace for seven weeks. As a result a few of the lads were, unsurprisingly, intimidated by him. When he walked into a room the atmosphere definitely changed, as you just didn't know what he would do next. He was completely unpredictable.

It is clear to me now that he must have been using drugs because a lot of the time he was completely spaced out. Back then I suppose we were a little naïve, and didn't really consider that a colleague might have an addiction problem. We just thought he was mad. For instance, in the Welsh Cup that year we met Shrewsbury Town in the

At Ninian Park, my spiritual home.
(*courtesy: Richard Shepherd*)

Battered and worn, a bit like me!
This is the only photo of me and
my Grangetown pals lining up for
Mostyn high school. I'm in the front
row, with the ball in my hands.

Getting ready for action
in my first year as a
professional.

MEET CARDIFF CITY'S F.A. YOUTH CUP STARS. (Back from left): Phil Dwyer, Jimmy Hobby, Billy Kelloch, Alan Shaw, John Williams, George Gibbs, Alan Couch, Nigel Rees. (Front): Derek Showers, Jimmy McInch, John Impey (captain), Bryan Rees.

The famous Cardiff City youth team, which reached the FA youth
cup final in 1971.

With the Wales youth team. I am in the front row, second from right, and on the end of the row is Peter 'Aberdare' Davies.

Celebrating winning a youth cap for Wales. *From left to right*: Yours truly, Nigel Rees, Alan Couch, Derek Showers, John Williams and Jimmy Hobby.

One of my trademark tackles, high and late without a ball in sight.

Celebrating a goal against Nottingham Forest in 1974.

Clearing my lines in a game against Derby County.

The Cardiff City first-team squad, just before the disastrous 1974/75 campaign, which saw the club relegated to the old third division. I am in the front row, third from left, between David Powell and Gil Reece.

The day I nearly died on a football pitch.
In an away game with Gillingham in season 1975/76 I swallowed
my tongue and was in some distress, with one reporter even
suggesting that I had passed away. Thanks to some smart work
by our physio, Ron Durham, I survived.

My lifesaver,
Ron Durham,
checks in on
Ann, my son
Darren and I
after my brush
with death.

Looking like extras from *Starsky and Hutch*, Freddie Pethard and I are happy with our duty-free purchases after playing Ferencvaros in the European Cup Winners Cup.

Dwyer the Dragon. I was always so proud to represent my country. Here I am with the Wales squad before winning my first cap against Iran, a game in which to my surprise and delight I scored the winner. I am sixth from the left in the back row.

We always had time for socialising and a good laugh.
Enjoying a round of golf with Ron Healey, Wayne Hughes,
Rod Thomas and Peter Grotier.

My wife Ann and I in the company of the great Welsh comedian,
Max Boyce. If we weren't laughing at his jokes we may have been
laughing at his perm!

I wasn't the most skilful player of all time but I always gave 100 per cent in that famous blue jersey. I hope this 1978 photograph of me bulleting home an Alan Campbell cross illustrates that commitment.

Down to business. In the front row, listening intently as manager Alan Durban addresses the players at Jubilee Park.

The south Wales derby is one of the most fiercely contested of all. Here I am bamboozling David Giles and John Toshack with my footwork.

Scoring against England. My joy was unconfined when I guided a header past the great
Peter Shilton in the home internationals of 1978. And to score it at Ninian Park
made it even more special.

*(courtesy Colorsport)*

Playing for Wales against Scotland and about to give Graeme Souness some of his own medicine.

The toughest game of my career was away to West Germany in a European Championship qualifier. Playing against the likes of Karl Heinz Rummenigge and Klaus Fischer (*pictured*) was a real eye-opener. Wales lost 5–1.

I have always had a great relationship with the Cardiff City fans, who I consider to be the best in Britain. So it was an honour to receive the player-of-the-year trophy from them. Next to me is David Tong who got the award for the most-improved player.

final. At Shrewsbury we lost 3–0 and after the game the players, management and directors went to a bar to drown our sorrows. Robin got smashed and was completely off it, even for him. Screaming obscenities at anyone unlucky enough to be near him he jumped up onto the pool table and started hitting people with the cue. Matters were made even worse when he grabbed some of the snooker balls and launched them at the directors. It was then that I started seriously to wonder if he had some sort of mental illness.

All the reservations we had about Robin as a person, however, were swept away on the football pitch, where he could be sensational. Not only was he big, strong and quick but he also had every trick, and then some, in his locker. He could do some incredible things with a ball. Allied to his skill he was incredibly tough and would give as good as he got. Defenders hated playing against Robin, as he could humiliate them with his trickery and would also think nothing of giving them a punch off the ball. His temper was, however, a major drawback because he was always getting himself sent off. He certainly had the talent to be one of the top players in the country, of that there is no doubt, but his lifestyle and temperament meant that he would never fulfil his potential.

On Robin's debut we beat Fulham at Ninian Park and he scored twice. The fans immediately took to football's version of the Sex Pistols, with his unkempt long hair hanging over his collar, his shirt hanging out of his shorts and his contempt for authority. Though Robin provided us with some much-needed flair we still sank into the bottom three.

At times he could be a liability, such as when he got sent off against Hereford, after which we went 2–0 down. Getting a result in such circumstances seemed hopeless, but we really grafted hard and Leo Sayer got us two vital goals which saw us nick a 2–2 draw. The only real surprise from that game was that Robin had managed to stay on the field for as long as he did. From the first minute he proceeded to punch and kick anyone who came near him. If he was playing today, with all the television cameras around, he wouldn't last five minutes.

We did, however, see the best of Robin in our next game, at home to Wolves. Losing 2–0, and with a good result a distant prospect,

Jimmy brought Robin on from the bench and his introduction immediately changed the game as he set up goals for Leo and Wenty to see us come back from a two-goal deficit for the second week running. Robin had run Wolves ragged, but it was so frustrating to see what a good player he could be only for him to then let himself down.

Every result was now vital as we entered the home stretch. We were still bobbing around the relegation zone and desperately needed to win games if we were going to have any chance of staying up. With a few games remaining we played Luton at Ninian Park and won 4–2. It was a game that summed Robin up. He was unplayable that day, scoring twice, but the match is probably best remembered for him sticking two fingers up at the Luton goalkeeper after one of his goals. It was a scene that made a great picture for the newspapers, but it led to him getting suspended.

Games were running out and we were faced with a really tough encounter at Brian Clough's Nottingham Forest. Against all odds we put in a great display and won the game thanks to another Leo Sayer goal. Leo, a local boy, was enjoying a great first full season in professional football and his form also saw him get capped for Wales. Our result at Forest turned out to be the last time that they lost a home game for two years as they went on to earn promotion, swiftly won the first division and then became back-to-back champions of Europe.

As had been the case in previous seasons, our fate went down to the wire. On the last day of the season we were left needing a point, against Carlisle United, if we were going to stay up. AC put us into the lead but Carlisle struck back within sixty seconds and there was a very nervous climax to the game as we defended for our lives. In the closing stages I was just trying to boot the ball as far away from our goal as possible. It certainly wasn't total football but in such circumstances you do whatever is necessary. When the referee blew the final whistle, after what seemed like an age, I was relieved. We had stayed up by the smallest of margins.

Our league campaign may have been disappointing but that was tempered by the run we had in the FA Cup. In the third round we got a great draw when we played first division Spurs at Ninian Park. Spurs had some good players, with the likes of Glenn Hoddle, Pat

Jennings and John Pratt in their ranks, but they were struggling in the league. Still, no one gave us a chance, but we caused a major shock when we beat them 1–0, thanks to another Leo goal.

In the fourth round we played our Welsh rivals, Wrexham, again at Ninian Park, in a game I will never forget. Gilo and Leo had put us two up but Wrexham equalised with two goals in the last few minutes. We looked to have thrown it away but in the final seconds of injury time Buchy popped up in the box. Keeping his cool he fired the ball into the corner of the net to win the game and send the 29,000 fans at Ninian Park home with a smile on their faces.

Everton were our opponents in the next round and it was great to face another top-flight club and test ourselves against the best. Over 35,000 fans turned up to watch the game and were thrilled when, against the run of play, Evo put us 1–0 up. Everton were a top side though, and while we competed well, their class eventually shone through and they went on to win the game 2–1. Losing was no disgrace and it was a real confidence booster to have played against two great teams like Spurs and Everton and never to have felt out of my depth.

All in all it had been a mixed season but after losing big players, such as Adrian Alston and Mike England, it was never going to be easy. The core of our squad was still good, with the likes of Doug Livermore, AC, Tony Evans, Willie Anderson and Peter Sayer, and I felt that it would only take a few additions to really get us going again.

# 10

# Taking it to the Wire

Over the previous two seasons we had been also rans in the second division, and even before the 1977/78 campaign got underway, it was clear to me that we were in for another long, hard struggle. Before the season had even begun the club was really up against it as the safety certificate for parts of Ninian Park was revoked, due to the new Sports Safety Act coming into force. This meant that Ninian Park was limited to a 10,000 capacity, and that we couldn't play night games, until the problems were rectified. At the time there was outrage, but being honest we struggled to get gates of anywhere near ten thousand in those days.

Football grounds were a real hazard at that time. There were no crash barriers, the stands were made of wood, huge crowds were crammed into pens, and, perhaps worst of all, there was no real crowd segregation, which led to running battles on the terraces. It was no real surprise that the authorities wanted to do something about it but it certainly left the club in a vulnerable position until it had been sorted.

To be honest, the players were a little worried at the way things were going. The club had been struggling financially, despite the takeover, and with the capacity at the ground being reduced we knew our gates could be severely affected. If the club wasn't taking as much money through the turnstiles, then not only could we not afford new players, but also some of us might have to be sold. Worst-case scenario, those that stayed might not even get paid wages.

None of us were on big money in those days; we all had families to support and mortgages to pay. Not getting paid would have been disastrous and it was certainly something that had me worried. It wasn't the best way to start a new season and, not surprisingly, a few of the boys were distracted. We wondered which direction the club was taking. Off the pitch it was clear that things were in a mess and I am sure we must have been on a financial knife edge. Whilst I fretted over the state of the club I don't think I ever considered for one moment that we could go under. Maybe I was being naïve, but, quite honestly, I could not comprehend Cardiff City not being around anymore.

Dicing with death during the previous season had made it obvious to everyone that things needed to change. With a limited transfer budget available I wasn't, however, holding my breath. I just hoped and prayed that we could keep our best players and perhaps add one or two useful recruits on free transfers. At no point was I expecting us to be involved in the promotion chase but I just hoped that we could be competitive, and hold off relegation, until the club got an injection of cash from somewhere.

Amidst all of these worries I was surprised to be offered a highly lucrative escape route. One day I was asked to contact an agent, who said he had something that might interest me. I forget his name now but I am sure he was a former first-division goalkeeper who was doing some scouting for foreign clubs. With nothing to lose I gave him a call, and was taken aback when he asked if I had ever considered playing abroad. I had to admit that it had never crossed my mind as I never thought that there was much call for a rugged centre half from Grangetown on the Continent! He proceeded to tell me that Greek giants Panathinaikos had been monitoring me and were keen to sign me.

Whilst I was flattered to hear that I was on the radar of a great club like Panathinaikos I have to admit that my initial reaction was that I didn't fancy leaving Cardiff. I had a young family that I didn't want to uproot, and I was more than happy realising my lifelong ambition of playing for my hometown club, in spite of its precarious financial position. However, when I was told what they were offering I have to admit that my head was turned. The actual figures

escape me now but the salary was far in excess of what I was earning at Cardiff, which wouldn't of course have been hard. I was also
told that Panathinaikos would provide me with a villa, and that they
would pay for my children to attend an English school in Athens. An
offer like that was one I had to take seriously.

Before I could take the matter any further I told the agent that
I needed to discuss it with my wife. I didn't have to twist her arm.
Ann was understandably thrilled at the prospect of more money and
a villa in the sun, so she gave the move the thumbs up. Even though
I was very tempted I still hadn't made my mind up. Cardiff City
weren't going anywhere fast, and I could have certainly done with a
bit more money, but they were *my* club and I loved playing for them.

If there was any prospect of the move happening I would need
to speak to Jimmy Andrews. To be honest I wasn't sure how Jimmy
would react. Part of me felt he might be glad to get some money
for me, but at the same time I always seemed to be one of the first
names on his team sheet, and he hardly ever had a bad word to say
to me. Any intention I may have had of speaking to Panathanaikos
was soon put in its place after Jimmy bluntly told me, 'No chance.
I'm not selling you.' In a strange way it was nice to hear that I was so
highly thought of by the manager. If I had really wanted the move to
go through I suppose I could have thrown the toys out of the pram
and dug in, but that wasn't my style and I was actually very happy
that Cardiff still wanted me.

Both Bristol City and Stoke also made bids to sign me that year
but Jimmy turned them both down point blank. Bristol were in the
first division, and had offered £150,000 for my services, a huge sum
of money at the time, but still Jimmy refused to budge. Of course the
prospect of playing in the top flight was a tantalising prospect, but I
wanted to do it with Cardiff City, so I can't say I was that tempted.

After all the uncertainty leading into the new campaign I tried
my best to focus. If we were going to have any chance of doing anything then all of our key players needed to be fit and firing. One of
those, a guy I pinned my hopes on, was the mercurial Robin Friday.
Unfortunately, Robin being Robin, he had gone AWOL, and while
the official line was that he had picked up an illness, and would be
back in a few weeks, I wasn't sure if we would see him again.

Jimmy Andrews had so much faith in Robin's ability, and he really went out of his way to get him to reach his potential, but I think he was now beginning to realise that it wasn't going to happen. The rough was now rapidly outgrowing the smooth and Jimmy was at the end of his tether. It seems mad to say this, as Jimmy was the manager, but I honestly think he was scared to have a blast at Robin because he knew that he would probably end up getting knocked out.

While Robin was absent Jimmy went out and signed Keith Robson from West Ham. I think Alan Sealey must have used his connections at Upton Park to snap him up. Robbo was a Geordie lad, who was a bit of a porker, but he could certainly play. We thought up some affectionate nicknames, such as 'Fat Bastard', but he gave as good as he got and he definitely had the potential to do well for us.

It came as no surprise that we struggled badly at the start of the season, winning just once in our first ten games. We couldn't even progress in Europe as we crashed out of the competition to those well-known giants of European football, Austria Memphis. Whatever happened to them?

One game that did, however, give us a boost came against the glamour boys of the league, Tottenham Hotspur. Spurs had been surprisingly relegated from the top tier of English football the previous season and everyone was keen to take their scalp. Although crowds had been poor during the first few games I was confident they would come flocking back to watch us take on Spurs. Unfortunately, I was wrong, because we couldn't even fill our limited-capacity ground. It was disappointing that so many fans had lost faith in us, but those who did come were tremendous and I think we gave them their money's worth. No doubt most of them thought we were in for a hiding, but we shocked just about everyone, including ourselves, when we earned a point in a hard-fought goalless draw. This certainly helped to give us some belief and I hoped that it could be a platform for us to push on up the table.

Just as we were trying to keep our focus on football off-field matters dominated our thoughts. Stefan Terleski, our chairman, had a falling out with directors Bob Grogan and Jack Leonard and as a result he stepped down. I was sad to see Stefan leave, as he was a Cardiff City fan who did his best with limited resources to keep the club afloat.

Perhaps a change at this point was, however, needed to reignite things and I was pleased to see Bob Grogan step up as chairman.

Bob Grogan was a very wealthy and ambitious man, who had the nous and resources to really make something of the club. The players were pleased as we hoped that the club would now be more secure and that in turn we wouldn't have to worry about our wages being paid. By now I was becoming immune to the constant off-field drama and had learnt to keep my head down and get on with the football, which after all was what I was being paid for. It was hard at times because there always seemed to be a distraction of some kind, but I knew I wasn't going to be able to change anything and so I focused all my efforts on Saturday afternoons.

With so much going on in the boardroom Robin Friday finally returned and I just hoped that his head was now on playing football rather than causing mayhem. If he was on song he could be invaluable, as we were still well down the league, and with the busy Christmas period approaching it was vital that we put a run together sooner rather than later.

His first game back came against Brighton on 29 October and Mark Lawrenson, future *Match of the Day* pundit, was given the unenviable job of marking him. It was obvious from the start of the game that both of them would be lucky to last the ninety minutes. Straight from kickoff they set about kicking lumps out of each other and I saw Robin smack Lawro off the ball a few times when the referee wasn't watching. Eventually he pushed his luck too far and received his marching orders. We were all furious, in particular Jimmy Andrews, whose faith in Robin had once again been thrown in his face.

Fighting hard for the majority of the game, with just ten men, away from home, was always going to be tough and it was no surprise when we ended up losing 4–0. What made matters worse was that when we returned to the changing room, expecting to see a contrite Robin offering us his apologies, he had scarpered. Jimmy Andrews finally lost it; in fact he went ballistic. I think it had finally dawned on him that no one was going to be able to get the best out of the enigmatic Robin Friday. He just upset everyone: the opposition, his teammates and the management although the fans loved him because it was clear that he could do things with a ball that most of us couldn't dream of.

Robin's Cardiff career didn't, however, end that day. Following a 6–1 loss, at home to Sheffield United, Jimmy Andrews decided to give him a final chance against Bolton Wanderers. It was a huge gamble but we were playing so poorly that I think Jimmy was getting desperate. To be fair to Robin he actually had a pretty good game against Bolton and concentrated more on kicking the ball than his opponents. He played better than most of us, which wasn't too hard, as we were well off the pace, and shipped six goals for the second game in a row. We were now well and truly up against it.

There had been plenty of opportunities for Robin to walk away from football during his time at Cardiff so I was stunned when he suddenly announced his retirement straight after the Bolton game. It seemed strange that after he had actually played well, and with no drama, he should choose this moment to pack it in. He was only in his mid twenties so I always thought that one day, after a break, he would make a comeback, but he was true to his word and never played another game of professional football.

In my time as a footballer I have been privileged to play alongside some very talented players but I don't think anyone has either excited, or infuriated, me as much as Robin. I would have killed to have half his skill, but he couldn't stay out of trouble and dedicate himself to the life you have to lead as a professional. If any case proves that talent can only get you so far in the game then this was it.

For a long time I didn't hear anything about Robin but in 1990 I was told that he had passed away at the age of thirty-eight. I was shocked he had died so young but the fact that drugs had played a part didn't surprise me. He always lived life on the edge and it was clear that if he carried on the way he was going then one day he was going to end up in serious trouble. Sadly, that proved to be the case.

Looking back now I realise he never had anyone he could turn to. It is clear that he was a very troubled young man, who needed a lot of guidance and help, and back then no one really understood his problems. At the clubs he played for he never made any close friends, in fact most players were so frightened of him they were glad when he left the room. Sometimes I wonder, could I have done more? Out of all of the lads I suppose I was the one who Robin would talk to, but, in all honesty, I don't think he would have listened to anything I had to say. He was a one off, a complete maverick, and he certainly lived his life the way he wanted to live it. It saddens me to this day to think of such a waste and I only hope that he has now found the happiness in death that he could never find in life.

With Robin gone, and the team shipping goals left, right and centre, Jimmy realised he needed to tighten us up. However, before he could bring in new players he had to sell so he decided to let Doug Livermore join Chester. It was a real shame to see Doug leave as he was a lovely player. In a good side he looked great, but in truth he was not cut out for a relegation battle, and we needed to bring in someone who would put their foot in.

To shore us up Jimmy signed Rod Thomas, a Wales international, from Derby. Rod was just the sort of player we needed at that moment in time. His steel and experience were vital attributes to help us stop the rot but even with him in the team we still couldn't manage to keep a clean sheet. Occasionally Tony Evans, or Peter Sayer, would get us out of trouble with a few goals but when you're conceding a minimum of two goals a match it is very difficult to pick up three points. Some games were truly embarrassing, we literally couldn't do anything right. There was a severe lack of confidence running through the squad. I suppose we all knew that this team wasn't good enough and even before a game had kicked off we had already lost it in our heads. Even the most talented players in the team started to suffer from a chronic lack of self-belief. We were sloppy at the back, losing the midfield battle and shot shy in front of goal.

Results continued to be poor over the Christmas period and for every good result, such as a 4–1 win over Millwall, we would then swiftly lose to the likes of Bristol Rovers. When a football club is in such disarray everyone feels the tension. No one likes getting hammered and no player ever truly believes that it is their fault. They will blame the manager, coaches, teammates, wife, kids, and even their dog, before they admit they haven't been doing the business. To survive in football a steely self-belief is just as vital as talent and that is the reason why few players hold their hands up when they haven't played well.

During our abysmal run of form, tempers finally came to a head following a 0–0 draw with Hull. Keith Robson and Alan Sealey, who had both joined from West Ham, had a punch up after the game in the club car park. Whilst I didn't actually witness the fight they were both outspoken characters and I can't say I was surprised. Robbo and Alan lived and breathed football and no doubt their pride was hurting at the state we were in. Both of them had strong views as to why we weren't picking up results and I think things finally exploded. There are always disagreements at football clubs, but usually it is kept in-house.

As this fight was in public it wasn't long before the story made its way into the local press. In order to calm things down Robbo and Alan kissed and made up at a press conference, but I think it was all for show as the two barely spoke after that. Shortly afterwards I wasn't surprised to see that Robbo was shipped off to Norwich. We all had strong views on the way things were going, but Robbo overstepped the mark by hitting one of the coaching staff. A player could not be seen to publicly undermine a coach and get away with it. If he had not been punished, or sold, then I have no doubt that other players would have thought it was acceptable to go about things in that manner. Robbo was a good player, and a great lad, but unfortunately he had to go.

Even a potential morale-boosting run in the FA Cup was out of the question as we lost to Ipswich, 2–0, in the third round. To be fair Ipswich were a leading first-division team in those days, boasting the likes of Arnold Muhren and John Wark in their ranks. Perhaps their star player was England forward, Paul Mariner, and he really proved his worth against us as he struck both goals. He ran rings around us that day and in the end I was thankful that they only scored the two as they were a far superior team.

The supporters had very little to shout about during this period and as a result our attendances started to plunge towards the six thousand mark. Over the last few seasons we hadn't given them any sign that we were going to improve and I think people just lost faith. The hardcore that continued to come to games were, however, fantastic, particularly those who travelled away. Our confidence was shot, but they never lost faith, sticking with us through thick and thin.

At times we didn't deserve their support. Some of those fans were spending their last pennies to watch us play and we very rarely repaid their efforts, yet they kept coming. It was tremendous and I know that whenever a new player signs for Cardiff he can never believe just how good our away support is. If you can't give those fans 100 per cent every time you pull on the blue shirt there is something wrong with you.

As the crowds plummeted, and our form continued to falter, I began to wonder how much longer Jimmy Andrews had left. Some of the more experienced players started to grumble that while he was a good coach, and they enjoyed training, he was not a great manager. It was hard for Jimmy as he had no money to spend, but every manager has a shelf life and I thought we needed someone to come in and give us a new lease of life. Perhaps the return of prodigal son John Toshack would be the answer and rumours swept the city that he was being lined up for a sensational appointment as player-manager.

Since 1970, when he had acrimoniously left Cardiff to join Liverpool, Tosh had gone on to forge one of the most feared strike partnerships in Europe alongside Kevin Keegan. The fans had continued to worship him and the thought that he could come back excited a lot of people. Despite this, I have to admit that I didn't think he was the man for the job. We were really struggling at this point and it would have been a hell of a gamble to appoint an inexperienced manager, like Tosh, when we were in a dogfight.

At one point Tosh did come down to discuss the possibility of a coaching role at the club. I don't know the ins and outs but it appears that Jimmy Andrews nipped his return in the bud. I think he must have realised that if Tosh came back in any capacity then there would be a clamour for him to take over as manager whenever we lost a game.

We all know now that, shortly thereafter, Tosh joined Swansea as player-manager and sensationally led them to the first division. Could he have delivered similar success at Cardiff? It is possible, because during the Eighties and Nineties he proved that it was no fluke as he established himself as one of the best managers in Europe and even enjoyed success at a massive club like Real Madrid. Hindsight is a wonderful thing and I suppose that if the club could go back, and make the decision again, they would definitely have appointed him.

There was no doubt that the speculation about Jimmy's position started to get to him, and with us failing dismally on the pitch, he threw his last roll of the dice. Out of nowhere he announced that the entire squad was up for sale. I think Jimmy thought that this move would mark a line in the sand. We either jumped ship at the earliest opportunity, revolted or played our hearts out to prove him wrong. In all honesty I remember thinking that we were all playing so poorly that no one would want us anyway. I think a lot of the lads felt the same and the announcement was met with complete bemusement. In the end I think Peter Sayer was the only player who left, joining Brighton for £100,000.

While we were initially sceptical of Jimmy's outburst it worked. We suddenly started to win games, beating Sunderland, Blackpool and Brighton in quick succession. Were we all suddenly putting more effort in after a kick up the backside? It's possible, but in my case I can honestly say that I continued to play just as I had done before. Maybe it wounded some of the lads' pride, and acted as a wake-up call. I can't honestly say, but for whatever reason we started to play well.

Although we won a few games we were really short on forwards as Robbo, Leo and Robin had all left, and Tony Evans had picked up an injury. With no money to spend Jimmy started to use either Paul Went or myself up front, to act as a target man, and get on the end of crosses. Neither of us was that mobile. I was probably quicker than Wenty – although he would definitely disagree with that assessment – but we both enjoyed our stint up top and notched some vital goals. Wenty struck to help us pick up points against Bristol, Oldham, Sunderland, Blackpool and Notts County while my goals saw us get results against the likes of Stoke, Burnley and Crystal Palace. I was never going to play there permanently but, incredibly, my performances at centre forward even earned me an international call up – of which more later – so I couldn't have done too badly.

Fighting for our lives, going into the final few games of the season, it still looked as if we would need a miracle to stay up. However, a surprise 1–0 win at home, against Bolton, gave us some belief and then anything seemed possible when Tony Evans scored a dramatic winner at Sheffield United. Other results went our way and with two games of the season remaining we were in an incredible position: just one win would be enough to guarantee safety. I don't think anyone could believe that we could still stay up after we had been so poor for the majority of the season.

The fans descended on Ninian Park, for our game against Notts County, and the stadium was close to capacity, which created a marvellous atmosphere. I remember that the sun was shining and that the fans were singing, 'Six foot two, Eyes of blue, Joey Dwyer's going to get you'. Hearing that song really fired me up and there was no way we were going to lose that day. Even though we went a goal down I had no doubt we would win. Everyone was playing with so much commitment, and the fans were so up for it. It was only a matter of time before Buchanan equalised. Just one more goal and the great escape would be achieved and it came through Paul Went, who was again deployed as a striker. What a relief it was when that ball hit the back of the net. I was too knackered to run over to Wenty to celebrate so I just turned to the Bob Bank and pumped my fists. Facing the crowd all I could see was a wave of people going mad. I remember that I stood in awe for twenty seconds and watched them. The joy on their faces is something I will never forget.

When the final whistle finally blew you would have thought we had won the cup. Hordes of fans ran onto the pitch and I think I grabbed Buchy and gave him a big kiss. At the turn of the year we had been favourites to go down but somehow we had survived. That night we drank the players' bar dry. While we had only avoided relegation, we were all so relieved that when it mattered we had stood up to be counted. We were far from the best team around but in those final few months we had shown enormous spirit and determination.

Football is funny. Although it was the game against Notts County that saw us avoid relegation the match most people want to talk to me about is our last game of the season, at home to Leyton Orient. Orient needed a win to stay up, and as we were already safe, we had nothing to play for. Looking back I think that our exploits against Bolton, Sheffield United and Notts County had left us drained and in that final game we were running on empty. It certainly showed as we started the game second best all over the pitch and Peter Kitchen, who would one day sign for Cardiff, put Orient into the lead.

Once Orient had their goal they sat back to defend and the game descended into a farce. We were knackered, and despite being behind, we couldn't get going. Our efforts were lacklustre to say the least. No one wanted to take any responsibility so we just passed the ball sideways and backwards. Orient let us get on with it and we rarely ventured over the halfway line. Some of the supporters became frustrated, and started to boo. I couldn't blame them as they had paid good money to watch a game of football, not a fiasco. The game ceased to be a contest and, to the sound of the crowd's displeasure, Orient won and stayed up.

Without a doubt it was one of the strangest matches I have ever played in. Over the years plenty of fans have suggested that it was a fix, and that we had thrown the game, but I swear that wasn't the case. I can't blame them for thinking that, as it was that bad, but if anyone did receive money then I certainly didn't see any. After the game there was even a bit of banter between the players, as Wenty used to play for Orient. I remember some of the lads saying 'Come on Wenty, how much did they pay you for that?' Wenty was too proud to ever consider doing such a thing and he used some choice language to have a pop at the rest of us.

It had been a strange season, full of highs and lows on the pitch, and plenty of drama off it, but somehow we had another season in the second division to look forward to. I just hoped that things would get sorted in the summer as I didn't think my heart could take any more of the Cardiff City rollercoaster.

# 11

# The Life and Times of a 1970s Footballer

You may have noticed that my life as a professional footballer was far removed from the luxury lifestyle that the players of today enjoy. Don't get me wrong, I was hardly living on the breadline, and enjoyed some nice perks, but I wasn't revelling in champagne or driving a Ferrari. In fact, the nearest I got to Ferrari's was when I used to visit the old bakery on Wellfield Road!

The prospect of owning a Ferrari, as a Championship footballer in my time, would have been very far-fetched. These days, it is almost the done thing for a footballer at that level to have a Ferrari, Bentley or Lamborghini. If you look at the cars parked outside the Cardiff City stadium today, you will see that even the reserve players own luxury motors that cost more than most people's annual salaries. The flashest car I owned as a player was my canary-yellow Ford Escort. That really was my pride and joy, despite the stick I got for it, and I had to stretch my finances to afford it.

In financial terms I wasn't badly off. At my peak I was earning around £250 a week, which wasn't to be sniffed at in those days. It would certainly have been above the average fan's salary but it wasn't enough to allow me to live a drastically different lifestyle. I don't know if I would have gone crazy, even if I had been earning big money. I have always enjoyed relatively normal things, such as playing and watching football, having a pint in the pub and going to Spain on holiday. I don't think any amount of money would have changed that.

My biggest extravagance as a player was buying my first home: a small, three-bedroom, semi-detached house in Llanedeyrn. I think the price was £12,000; you would be lucky to get a shed for that money now. Llanedeyrn is of course a decent, working-class area, but you wouldn't expect to see a professional footballer living there today. I definitely can't imagine Jay Bothroyd doing his weekly shop in the Maelfa shopping centre like I used to.

Players can now afford to live in gated mansions and therefore have very little day-to-day contact with the fans. Being in Llanedeyrn meant that I was living next door to Cardiff City supporters, and I couldn't step outside my front door without someone wanting to speak to me about the game. If I was out the front, mowing the lawn, all sorts would stop for a chat. I'm lucky, as I have always loved talking about football, so it was never an issue for me, although Ann would be annoyed as it would take me hours to get the lawn finished.

Most weekends I would go up the road, to the Pennsylvania pub, for a pint with John Buchanan, and although fans would have a chat with me, I never felt harassed. If Craig Bellamy went for a quiet drink in a local pub today I'm sure it would be a little different. In fact there would probably be pictures of him all over the internet within minutes of him sitting down.

By and large I was left in peace when I was out but there was one incident that almost got out of hand. I was in the pub one evening, chatting to a group of fans, when out of nowhere some drunken idiot squared up to me, and said in an aggressive tone, 'Why do you keep looking at me funny?' It was obvious he was plastered so I politely explained that I wasn't looking at him, and that he should leave me alone. However, he was determined to make a name for himself, and quickly became very abusive. Just as I was about to really lay into him he suddenly dropped to the floor. One of the guys I had been speaking to had chinned him. I was amazed and I just stood there, open-mouthed, unable to take it in. Then my 'protector' explained why he had done it: 'No one speaks to Phil Dwyer like that,' he informed me. During my career I had always taken care of my own problems but it was certainly nice to know that the fans would look after me if there was any trouble.

These days the players have to be so careful about what they say and where they go. They are under constant scrutiny. If they step ever so slightly out of line it will hit the headlines. Recently Craig Bellamy was involved in a spot of trouble in Cardiff city centre and it made the national news. In my day there were plenty of punch ups when we went out and it wouldn't even make the local paper. Robin Friday couldn't go a day without slapping someone when he was out and I dread to think what would happen if he was playing today.

The much greater media focus on football means that the players also have to be careful who they speak to. When I met the fans I knew we could have a proper chat, safe in the knowledge that what we discussed wouldn't get any further than a couple of their mates. Today, however, internet message boards, and social-networking sites such as Twitter, mean that a fan can broadcast a conversation to thousands of people. Before you know it you've got yourself, and the club, into trouble.

It has been well documented that former manager Dave Jones cracked down on which subjects the players, and staff, could talk about. The problem was that details of their conversations were being leaked onto the internet, and were then being broadcast by the media. I am sure the players were quite innocently chatting to friends, without ever intending their comments to go any further, but there is such interest in the game now that any story regarding a footballer is newsworthy. Unfortunately, it means that players feel that they can't speak to anyone. I am in no doubt that some of them would love to chat to the fans about the ins and outs of the club but it's not worth the hassle they would get. It is sad they can't speak openly but times have changed. If half the things I told fans during my playing days had been broadcast I would have been in very hot water indeed.

After a game at Ninian Park the players would always enjoy a pint with supporters in the John Charles suite. If someone approached me to discuss the game I would be happy to talk about how we had played, what had gone right, or wrong, and what we would look to do in the next fixture. I never pulled my punches. If someone had a shocker, including myself, I would say so. In the new stadium I know that the players no longer have any contact with fans in the bar after the game. It's straight in for a shower, into their car and off home. If someone is lucky enough to bump into a player an in-depth discussion is out of the question, simply because he has his guard up.

Through no fault of their own the players are often accused of being detached from the average fan. However, the salaries these guys are earning means that they don't live like the average fan, and therefore can't be expected to really understand or relate to them. They don't live in the same areas, they don't go to the same places and they don't do the same things; so contact is minimal.

It was highly unusual for me to go a day without speaking to a fan when I was playing. Even when I was on holiday I would bump into Cardiff City supporters. More often than not I spent my summers in self-catering accommodation in Benidorm. I would muck in, helping to cook the food, and would then spend most days building sandcastles with the kids. We loved it and I look back on those trips with very fond memories. This was also the type of foreign holiday the fans themselves went on and nearly every time I was away I would be stopped on the beach for a chat. Holidays for the player of today consist of first-class travel and a five-star hotel, in luxury destinations such as Dubai. It is the sort of trip most fans can't even dream about.

Going on a night out is also a vastly different experience for the modern footballer. They walk straight to the front of the nightclub queue and receive VIP treatment in a private room. In my day, when the players and their wives went out, we usually headed to Tito's, on Greyfriars Road, and not only did we not receive any VIP treatment but also we were lucky to even get in! The likes of Max Boyce and Tommy Cooper could stroll in while the City players would be left to queue like everyone else.

Footballers weren't treated like huge stars back then. Yes, we got some attention but we weren't followed by paparazzi and hounded for autographs. People would say hello but they wouldn't fall over themselves when they bumped into you. Seldom was the time I received any additional benefit for being a footballer. If I was in Cardiff central market one of the barrow boys would occasionally throw me a bag of fruit and just to get that was a genuine thrill. I was an ordinary bloke who played football, and the idea that people would give me things for free because of my job seemed ludicrous.

Nice perks are part and parcel of being a player today. I know that some can now go into a trendy boutique and the owner will give them free clothes, just so they can say that a player shops in their store. If I had gone into the old Mackross, or Marment's, department stores on Queen Street, and asked for free clothes, just because I was a footballer, they would have laughed in my face.

If I had ever tried to use my so-called fame to get anything I would have been on a hiding to nothing. Despite becoming a footballer, and moving to Llanedeyrn, I still kept in touch with my old mates from Grangetown. When we hit the town together, they would sometimes try to get to the front of a queue, or get served quicker, by pointing at me and asking, 'Don't you know who he is?' I would flash a smile, waiting to be recognised, but invariably I would be told to bugger off.

Things that are taken for granted today, such as sponsorship, which virtually every professional player has in some shape or form, were alien to me in my time at Cardiff City. I had to buy all my own gear and there was no chance of a sponsored car. The only player who got anything decent was Peter Sayer, who received a Triumph TR-7 after scoring against Spurs in the FA Cup.

Even shirt sponsorship didn't really catch on until the 1980s, and when it did the players didn't see a penny. The only time we ever got anything for shirt sponsorship was when a company asked to sponsor our shirts, on a purely one-off basis, for a game against Swansea. As this sort of thing was virtually unheard of we didn't know how to react so I told the company, and the club, that we would only wear the shirts if the players were given £200 to share between us. There was outrage, and talk of player power gone mad, but we held firm. In fact we only agreed to wear the shirts just five minutes before kickoff, after the chairman had entered the changing room, and had reluctantly given us a brown paper bag with our money inside it.

Negotiating deals was something I had to do for myself when I was playing. There were no agents or lawyers to turn to. The first player I knew who had an agent was Billy Ronson and I remember we all thought he was mad. Back then the clubs were all powerful, and it wasn't until the Bosman ruling came into force – which allowed a player freedom of movement when his contract had expired – that players had a card to play in negotiations. If a club told you that you were staying put, and that you would receive a certain salary, that was pretty much it, and you were grateful for it.

It is great that in the modern game players have people they can turn to for advice. After all, it is a short career, and you have to make the most of it while you can. There are so many distractions today that you seem to need an adviser for everything, from handling the media to dealing with your finances. It is a minefield and in a way I am glad that it was a lot simpler when I was in my prime. I just wanted to play football without any distractions.

Earning just above the average wage, and with very few perks, Ann certainly didn't enjoy the WAG lifestyle. But even if I had been earning mega money, I don't think that would have been her thing. She has always been very down to earth, and enjoys working, and she wouldn't have been the type to shop all day, and seek fame. Material possessions have never been the be all and end all for her, and during my playing career she even continued to work as a receptionist at the Angel hotel. For over twenty years she has worked as an assistant in a care home, and has also helped out at a local nursery. If there was ever any danger of me getting carried away with myself she would soon bring me back down to earth.

A big night out for the two of us would be a trip to the old Odeon cinema on Queen Street. Usually she would pick the film, which meant I would have to endure something girly. One time, however, I got to choose, so we went to see *Star Wars*. I loved it but the look on her face clearly told me that she wasn't a fan of Yoda and Darth Vader.

After a film, if I was flush, I would treat Ann to a slap-up meal at either Le Napoleon, in the Oxford Arcade, or La Corona on Newport Road. I enjoyed tucking into a classic 1970s three-course meal, which consisted of prawn cocktail, steak and chips and Black Forest gateau for dessert. You wouldn't get very far asking for fancy dishes, such as sushi, in those days. If we ever fancied something more low key we always enjoyed going to the Grotto, near Roath Park Lake. It really was a grotto as well, just a long, narrow, dimly lit room but the food was always good.

When the boys at Cardiff City wanted to socialise together it was always unobtrusive. We may have had a round of golf, or a pint, but it was never anything flash. In the Seventies the city of Cardiff was hardly synonymous with a glitzy lifestyle. If we wanted to live it up our only choices were between Tito's, which boasted a casino and a disco, as well as the infamous Africa Room, or Bumpers in the Castle Arcade. However, you were more likely to see us enjoying a fry up in the Black and White café in Grangetown!

Sometimes I look at how the modern footballer lives and I think it must be great. But at the same time I wouldn't change a thing from my own career. Of course it would have been nice to have earned tens of thousands of pounds a week but I didn't do too badly. I could walk the streets without any hassle and I could happily chat away to fans for hours. I don't know if I could have put up with being hidden away all the time, feeling as though I had to watch every word that came out of my mouth. Some things have changed for the better, and some haven't, but all in all I am grateful for what the game has given to me.

# 12

# The Right Direction?

During the summer of 1978 a lot of work was done to get Ninian Park up to scratch. The old wooden Grange End was subsequently demolished and replaced by a smaller concrete terrace. I was sad to see it go, as that was where I had watched a lot of games in my childhood, but by all accounts it was a safety hazard and the club didn't have much choice. At least now Ninian Park satisfied the Sports Safety Act and we no longer had to operate with a limited capacity.

Bob Grogan also decided to back Jimmy Andrews in the transfer market and it finally looked as if the club was heading in the right direction. Everyone connected with Cardiff City was thrilled, and surprised, when we proceeded to spend a club record £75,000 on Newcastle's Mickey Burns, who joined us as a player-coach. Mickey had enjoyed success at both Blackpool and Newcastle and in his prime was regarded as one of the most exciting players in the country. He was not only quick, with an eye for goal, but he was also very skilful. The fact that in addition he was joining us as a coach was very intriguing and I looked forward to playing, and working, with him.

Splashing the cash, Jimmy also spent £65,000 on Wales international, Dave Roberts. It was great to see the club finally making waves in the transfer market but while Mickey's signing made sense to me I wasn't too sure about Dave. I knew him from the Wales under-21 squad and he was a lovely bloke and a decent centre half. However, in my eyes he was never worth that amount of money. He was skilful, good on the ball, but he wasn't the hardest player and in all honesty he wasn't any better than what we already had. To make way for Dave, Paul Went was sold, which surprised me, as Wenty had been invaluable for us the previous season. He had scored some vital goals and had also put his head in where it hurt at the back. Maybe Jimmy thought that Dave was more cultured, and was trying to get us to play more football, but for that amount of money the move didn't make sense to me.

We started the season with a 2–2 draw against Preston, and not only was I happy with the point, but I was also delighted to score my first goal of the season. Unfortunately, it proved to be a false dawn as we then won only one out of our opening seven matches, our nadir coming when we were thumped 7–1 by Luton. Everything that could have gone wrong that day did. They should have put fifteen past us. I think they hit the woodwork three or four times and Keith Barber, who was actually from Luton, made some superb saves to keep the score down.

The day after that 7–1 thrashing I went to the Pennsylvania Pub, with my father-in-law, for our usual Sunday pint, and it was like walking into a bar in the Wild West. As soon as I was through the door everyone's eyes were on me and I could sense a few people talking about my performance the previous day. I tried my best to ignore them, strode to the bar and ordered a pint. Obviously frustrated, the barman, a mad City fan, shouted at me, 'How can you show your face in public after yesterday?' There was a deathly hush; everyone was waiting for me to speak. After a moment's thought to find the right words, I finally announced, 'We were robbed.' That seemed to break the ice, because everyone laughed, but I was still hurting and felt humiliated.

Cardiff is a football-mad city and if you are on the wrong end of a drubbing you can expect the fans to give you stick if they see you out. Some of my teammates chose to lock themselves away, and wouldn't even go out to get a pint of milk, while others, like me, tried to grin and bear it. I would never have dreamt of hitting the town after a poor result, but I wasn't afraid to go about my daily business. To be honest, I always wanted to hear what people were saying because sometimes you can become detached living in the footballer's bubble. Most of the time the fans were great, and had nothing but kind words, but on the odd occasion I was given both barrels.

Everyone expected Mickey Burns to set us alight but I think it's fair to say that he didn't justify the hype. On the pitch his form was patchy and he failed to make a significant contribution. Nor did he add anything new as a coach. The fact that he was still a player meant that he wasn't too sure what sort of relationship he could have with his team-mates. Some of the lads felt that as he was part of the management team they couldn't speak when he was around as he might go back and tell Jimmy what they had said. Micky tried his best to be friendly, and there was never a time where it was proved that he did snitch on anyone, but I don't think he knew when to keep his distance and that made some of the lads uncomfortable around him.

With the team struggling, and our big-money signings failing to spark, Jimmy dropped both Dave Roberts and Micky for our next game against Blackburn. It was a brave decision as not only had he recently spent a lot of money on them but I also believe that Bob Grogan had used his contacts in the north-east to get Micky, and had signed him over Jimmy's head. The decision to drop him could have been seen as questioning the chairman's authority but to be fair to Jimmy he didn't have much choice. Micky wasn't producing the goods, and the team was at the wrong end of the table, so he had to do something, and fast.

Replacing Micky, against Blackburn, was a gangly, awkward striker called Gary Stevens, who we had recently signed from non-league Evesham for £3,000. Gary was a lanky streak of nothing, but he was hungry to succeed, worked hard and was a decent finisher. He certainly had a debut to remember as he scored the opening goal in our 2–0 win. Another player who did well against Blackburn was local lad, and defender, John Lewis, who was only at the club on a part-time contract, but would, in time, make a big impact for us. Micky wasn't best pleased at being left out and it came as no surprise that he left the club shortly afterwards. Thankfully, the club recouped the money they had spent on him, as they managed to sell him to Middlesbrough for £75,000. It was a move that suited both parties. Micky actually went on to score plenty of goals back in the north-east, but for whatever reason his time in south Wales didn't work out.

After the Blackburn victory we had some good results against the likes of Wrexham and Leicester, with Gary Stevens continuing to get his name on the score sheet. Despite our upturn in form we crashed 3–0 at Newcastle and were then swiftly beaten 4–1, at Ninian Park, by Charlton Athletic. Two days after the Charlton game Jimmy Andrews was sacked. I wasn't surprised to be honest. Results had been indifferent for a while and despite having had money to spend in the summer we weren't any better than the previous season. Perhaps Bob Grogan was also angry with Jimmy's treatment of Mickey Burns, but either way results had been poor for a while and I thought that a change could do us some good.

Grogan had plenty of contacts in football and I hoped that he would be able to bring in an established manager who would get us firing. With this in mind I don't think that anyone, in a million years, could have guessed who Bob had in mind for the position. Completely out of the blue, and in a move that shocked every Cardiff City fan, and player, Richie Morgan was appointed as caretaker manager. Richie had been with the club, as a player, for a good few years, but he had never really established himself. In fact, he had probably played more times for the reserves than anyone else ever had. Although he was still registered as a player I don't think he had played for quite some time as his main role appeared to be doing commercial work for the club.

Richie was a solid pro, who was well liked, but he never struck me as management material. I have to admit, I was a little disappointed that the club had missed the opportunity to bring in a manager with a solid track record. I consoled myself with the thought that Richie was likely to be a temporary solution and that maybe someone else was in the pipeline.

Knowing that his appointment wasn't universally popular Richie immediately called a meeting with the players. Fair play to him, he was excellent. He told us that while he appreciated he wasn't every-one's first choice as long as we did the business for him he would look after us. 'We are all in this together,' he said, 'and we all need to stand up and be counted.' The players were impressed, and a little surprised, as Richie really spoke and acted the part. True to his word he went out of his way to sort out the players and that motivated everyone want to give their all. If we ever had a problem we knew we could go to him and he would speak to the chairman on our behalf.

It was only little things really, but we appreciated it and he earned our respect.

Although Richie was well liked it still took him a while to find his feet. He was appointed in early November but we didn't win a game until 23 December 1978, against Fulham, and even that result was followed by 5–0 defeats to Brighton and Cambridge. I will always remember the Cambridge game as to me it showed Cardiff fans at their best. We were getting absolutely hammered and the weather was atrocious. Our poor fans were in an uncovered stand so they were also getting soaked, but rather than abuse us a load of them took off their tops and started doing the conga in the rain. They must have seen me laughing at them because all of a sudden the whole stand started chanting at me, 'Joey, stop the rain, Joey, Joey, Stop the rain!' It certainly helped to lift the gloom and on the coach, on the way home, the players couldn't stop talking about it. They had every right to slag us off but they kept supporting us. They were tremendous. Absolutely tremendous!

While we had the best fans in the league we certainly didn't have the best team and once again we found ourselves not only in the relegation zone but also out of the FA Cup, after a 3–0 defeat to Swindon. Just as it looked as if our slump was terminal we got lucky. Due to freezing conditions – and at a time when under-soil heating was a rarity – we didn't play a game for six weeks. This gave Richie the opportunity to really settle into the job, assess the squad and put us through a mini pre-season.

Back then we didn't have the benefit of state-of-the-art indoor training facilities, like the Vale, so we had to train wherever we could. Most days we would turn up at Ninian Park not having a clue where we would be going. Richie would frantically ring facilities all over south Wales to see if anywhere was available while we kicked our heels in the changing room. If nowhere could be found we would run up and down the steps of the grandstand but even that was hazardous as it was covered in ice. More often than not we trained on the old gravel car park opposite the ground.

One thing that had been obvious in Richie's first few weeks as manager was that he needed to bring in some coaches to give him a hand. He had tried to take training himself, but his approach was a bit old fashioned, and we spent more time running than we did work-ing with the ball. In an inspired move he brought back some old faces and they really lit up the place. Doug Livermore and Brian 'Hooky' Harris returned and they both became invaluable. Not only did we respect them for what they had done in their careers at Cardiff, and elsewhere, but they were also vastly experienced – and bubby char-acters to boot. Their presence gave us a new lease of life and training went up a notch as well. Doug was a fantastic coach and it was soon clear that he had found his calling. We spent a lot of time working with the ball, and on our shape, and it was no surprise to me that he went on to have a very successful career as a coach at top clubs such as Spurs.

While Brian and Doug thoroughly drilled us, Richie scoured the league for bargains to improve the squad. His first signing was Colin Sullivan, who he bought from Norwich for £70,000. Colin was a little full back with a sweet left foot and a great engine, but when I think of him the first thing that comes to mind is his accent, which was like the proverbial farmer Giles. The poor bloke couldn't open his mouth without one of us mimicking him. Richie's next signing is one that most City fans will remember – when Ronnie Moore joined us for £100,000, from Tranmere Rovers. Ronnie had enjoyed a fan-tastic scoring record at Tranmere and we all thought that signing him was good business. If truth be told, the move turned into a bit of a nightmare, but more on that later.

After six weeks without football we were all straining at the leash to get back into action. Doug and Brian had us well drilled, and we had also added Colin and Ronnie to the squad. We felt like a new team and for some reason I thought we would be okay, despite our precarious league position. Our first game back saw us kick off with a 1–0 win over Orient and we quickly followed that up with victories over Blackburn, Leicester and Newcastle. The match at Blackburn proved how far we had come. Linden Jones received his march-ing orders early on so we played most of the game with ten men. Conditions were horrendous, with the pitch covered in snow and a gale swirling, but we performed magnificently and won 4–1.

Slowly, but surely, we climbed out of the relegation places, but our record signing, Ronnie Moore, was having a bad time. He had been bought to score goals but it wasn't happening for him. There was no question that he was working his socks off, and getting into some great positions, but no matter what he did he just couldn't stick the ball in the back of the net. It was amazing, as he was lethal in training, but out on the pitch nothing would go right. At Tranmere he had shown that he was a goal scorer, but at Cardiff it was almost as if he was cursed. Expecting more of a return for £100,000 some of the fans got on poor Ronnie's back. It was obvious to the players and to the fans that he was a good bloke, who was working really hard, but he just wasn't getting any luck. If he had an open goal the ball would bobble at the vital moment and he would end up sticking it over the bar. Despite his barren spell he actually became a bit of a crowd favourite and when he finally scored, in a 3–1 win over Brighton, Ninian Park erupted. After that some supporters started to wear badges proclaiming, 'I Saw Ronnie Moore Score'. Some of the players got them too, and, although Ronnie laughed it off, I don't think he was best pleased. I am sure he was hurting inside and was desperate to do well.

Most of the players at the club were used to being in a relegation dogfight but this year, as we entered the final few games, we actually started to look up the table, rather than down. By now we were really playing well and we hammered Sheffield United, with Buchy getting a hat-trick, before getting the result of the season, a 2–1 win against Sunderland at Roker Park. That result stopped Sunderland going up and it really pleased Bob Grogan and Jack Leonard, who were mad Newcastle fans. In fact they were so happy that we all stayed in Newcastle after the game and the chairman took us out for a meal at a posh hotel. He happily told us, 'Eat and drink as much as you want lads, you deserve it.' We couldn't believe it and everyone had a great night, although when I saw the rest of the lads tucking into steak and lobster I immediately regretted my decision to experiment with frog's legs!

The trip to the north-east wasn't just a success on the football front. The day before the game we had gone to a racecourse to watch one of the chairman's horses run. Before the race Bob advised us to back his horse as he said it was in good form and likely to win. We all put on a few bob and lo and behold it romped home. We returned to

Cardiff with two points, a hangover and a few quid in our pockets. Happy days!

Over the final eleven games of the season we went unbeaten and signed off with a 1–0 win over Wrexham. Unbelievably, we finished in ninth place, and if the season had continued I have no doubt we would have been troubling the promotion spots. Tony Evans, Gary Stevens and John Buchanan were scoring freely and we were also tight at the back. I like to think I was showing some of my best form during this spell. Richie Morgan had done a fantastic job to get us playing as we did and we all took our hats off to him.

With a young, ambitious and successful manager, a balanced squad and a supportive, wealthy chairman, Cardiff City's future finally looked bright. I was certain we were going places.

# 13

## Dwyer the Dragon

Playing for my hometown club was something I had always fantasised about and I felt the same way about representing my country. Never in a million years did I think that I would be selected for Wales. If getting the chance to play professional football catapulted me into dream world then walking out in the red shirt of my country was a prospect that seemed laughable. Yet, despite my self-doubt, I managed to win ten caps and I cherished every single one of them.

My first call up came in 1978 and it was a bolt from the blue. Jimmy Andrews called me into his office one day after training and told me that I had been selected to play for Wales, against Iran, in Tehran. I honestly thought it was a wind up, particularly when he said that Mike Smith, the Wales manager, wanted me to play as a forward!

Playing international football is the pinnacle of any player's career, a real honour, and the fact that Mike Smith felt my form was good enough for Wales was such a thrill. I can't tell you how happy I was. Meeting up with the rest of the Wales squad, at their base in Newport, really highlighted the calibre of player I would be rubbing shoulders with. Alongside me in the squad were Terry Yorath, Dai Davies, Leighton Phillips, Leighton James, Joey Jones, Mickey Thomas and Alan Curtis. All of these guys had played, or would go on to play, at the top level and would enjoy marvellous careers. It is a wonder that Wales didn't achieve more with such a stellar line up.

I was so excited at being called up that I hadn't given much thought to the prospect of going to Iran. In my younger days I struggled to get out of Grangetown let alone go to the other side of the world, and while Cardiff's exploits in Europe meant I had done a bit of travelling, I had never been as far afield as the Middle East. The prospect certainly intrigued me, not only the place itself, but also because I wasn't even aware that Iran had an international team.

Tehran was like no place I had ever seen. Buildings of all shapes and sizes sprawled in every direction while bazaars and beggars bombarded my senses, as did the fruity smell of the tobacco pipes that everyone seemed to be smoking outside the cafes. Far from being restricted, as I had expected, the women wore what they liked and we were pleasantly surprised to see that alcohol was for sale.

After my experiences on the Continent with Cardiff I was holding my breath when it came to our hotel accommodation and the food. Mike Smith was in fact so worried by what might be on offer that he insisted the FAW fly a chef out with us. To my surprise, and delight, the hotel was really quite decent. It was clean, and had all of the amenities that you would expect, and it certainly beat some of the places that I had stayed at in Eastern Europe, which made Fawlty Towers look like a luxury resort.

Terry Yorath was my roommate for the trip, which I was happy with, as I don't think I could have roomed with someone like Leighton James. Leighton is a good guy but he's not someone you want to be with 24/7 as he just doesn't shut up and is so opinionated. Leighton is like Marmite for most people; you either love him or hate him. When I played against him I always used to enjoy kicking him. He would have a moan and that would only make me kick him even harder. I remember one time – shortly after we had played together for Wales – we came head to head in the south Wales derby. At one point I scythed him down, and as he lay on the floor he complained bitterly.

'For fuck's sake, Phil. We're teammates.'

'Not today we're not,' I replied, with a touch of menace in my voice.

Despite our tussles on the field I have never had any problems with Leighton and to be fair he can be very entertaining company.

I had definitely got lucky with Terry as my roommate, as we not only got on very well, but as he was also from Cardiff he was a huge City fan. While I wanted to hear the gossip from his club, Leeds

United, he was desperate for me to tell him all about what was happening at Cardiff. It was strange; Terry was a big-time footballer, playing for one of the country's leading clubs, yet he treated me with so much respect because I played for his beloved Cardiff City.

In spite of the squad containing plenty of current, and ex, Cardiff and Swansea players, we all got on very well. I know the supporters would like to think that we hated each other but people like Alan Curtis became one of my best friends in football, as did some of the others with Swansea connections. When you come together to play for your country you have to put club rivalry aside for the greater good. However, if any ardent Cardiff fans asked me what people like Leighton or Alan were like I would tell them, 'He's a Jack bastard,' just to keep them sweet.

On the day of the game I was understandably nervous, particularly when we arrived at the stadium to find over one hundred thousand crazed Iranians jumping around like maniacs. I spotted a Welsh flag in the stands and that really fired me up to do well for those who had made the incredible effort to come and watch us. Before kickoff Mike Smith, who was methodical in his ways – almost like a schoolteacher in fact – reminded us what our jobs were. As I was playing up front he told me that my job was to hold the ball up, lay it off to the midfield or the wingers, and then pop up in the box to get on the end of crosses. It seemed simple enough, but all thoughts of the game went out of my mind as we walked out of the tunnel. The cheering was so loud that the ground vibrated, it sounded like a hundred fighter jets were soaring over us. I felt a long way from Cardiff.

Early in the game I had a few good touches and that settled me down. In a strange way it also helped that my usual position was in defence as I knew the areas that defenders didn't want to be in. That knowledge allowed me to drag the Iranian defenders out of their comfort zone a few times and created space for the likes of Alan, Terry and Leighton to run into.

Despite not knowing anything about Iranian football, and being unable to name any of their players, they were actually a decent team. Technically, they were excellent and they were used to playing in the blazing heat, so at times they made life difficult for us. The game was balanced on a knife edge but in the second half I was presented with my only opportunity of the game, and I took it. I had scored for Wales on my debut. I went bloody nuts. The stadium went deathly quiet and all anyone could hear was me screaming over and over again, 'Get in there!'

As there was no television coverage only those present in the stadium witnessed my goal. Over the years I've got away with telling everyone that it was a screamer from forty yards that almost tore the net off. In truth it was a tap in, which my wife could have stuck away in her high heels, but I didn't care. I had scored for Wales. No one could ever take that away from me. What a feeling it was. Here I was, a boy from Grangetown, scoring for Wales in Tehran.

My goal turned out to be the winner and after the game the boys gave me a pat on the back. I can remember sitting in the changing room in shock. If anyone had told me just a few months before that I would play for Wales, up front, and score on my debut I would never have believed them.

I suppose I must have got a bit carried away because on the plane home I felt like a big time Charlie. Everyone was getting stuck into beers and champagne and I was really knocking them back. If you can't enjoy moments like that then what's the point? For the whole nine-hour flight home Terry, Dai Davies and I drank the trolley dry. By the end of the flight I was paralytic and I remember I woke up curled into a ball on the floor of the toilet cubicle. I didn't have a clue what had happened, but when I opened the door the plane was empty. When we had landed everyone had got off, completely forgetting about yours truly. I looked, and felt, an absolute state and I have no idea how I got home.

Following my match-winning performance against Iran I was thrilled to be selected for that summer's home internationals. In those days the home-international tournament was a big deal and the rivalry between the fans and players was great. England and Scotland could both call on world-class players and I couldn't wait to pit my wits against them.

Wales's first game in the 1978 tournament was against England at Ninian Park. The thought of playing against England, at my home ground, had me really excited. I was born within walking distance of Ninian Park and I know it's an overused cliché, but it really was a dream come true. When I stopped to think that just a few years previously I had been playing youth-team games on that pitch and now I would be playing for Wales, rubbing shoulders with the likes of Kevin Keegan and Peter Shilton, it blew my mind.

The one thing that I have, and will always remember, of the day we played England, was being on the team coach going down Sloper Road. When the supporters saw us there was a huge cheer and out of the corner of my eye I saw a fan holding up a large banner with the words 'Dwyer the Dragon' written on it. The sight of that brought a lump to my throat. I actually had to stop myself from crying in front of the lads I was so choked. Ninian Park was filled to the brim yet I could make out all of my family members, who were sitting in the grandstand. I think they were even more excited than me, if that was possible. All of them – my parents, brothers, wife and parents-in-law – had been with me since I was an apprentice. It had been a long journey to get to this point but I really wanted to make the day as memorable as possible for them all.

Singing the national anthem, before the game, was something that will stay with me forever. I always feel emotional singing the Welsh anthem anyway but to be singing it at Ninian Park, in a Wales jersey, was extra special. Unlike some international footballers today, who shall remain nameless, I sang with real gusto and belted it out. We all did. Every one of us was so proud and the Wales international anthem is one that, when sung properly, electrifies a stadium.

Once again I was selected to play upfront and Mike Smith told me to do the same as I did against Iran. Obviously, England were a far superior team to the Iranians but I just played my natural game and ruffled a few feathers early on with some hard but fair challenges, particularly on Trevor Cherry, who had to leave the game on a stretcher after he went up for a header with me.

I remember the first time I got the ball there was a huge cheer from the Cardiff supporters and that really got me going. However, despite everyone being so pumped up we swiftly fell behind to a Bob Latchford goal. At times we were chasing shadows, as England were really on song, and I began to fear that we could be on the end of a thumping.

On a rare break, in the second half, Carl Harris went on a mazy run and got himself to the by-line. I knew he was going to try and clip a ball to the back post so I darted into that area and hoped that he could find me. As the ball was chipped in I used every ounce of strength that I had to leap above my marker, snap my head back and meet the ball as forcefully as I could. Falling backwards everything seemed to happen in slow motion as I watched the ball go beyond Peter Shilton's outstretched hand and towards the top corner.

Goal! I had done it!

Ecstatically, I ran away to celebrate, but I still had time to look back and shout, 'Don't worry Shilts, the net will stop it.' I couldn't believe this was happening to me. Two goals in two games for Wales and I had just scored against England, and at Ninian Park of all places.

Although England won the game 3–1, thanks to two late goals, I couldn't wipe the smile off my face. Without a doubt that goal is one of my most cherished memories in my time as a professional foot-baller. If I could have picked a fixture I would want to score in, Wales versus England, at Ninian Park, would have been right up there.

There was little time to mark the occasion, with family and friends, as the next morning the squad was whisked off to Scotland to prepare for our second game. Scotland had an awesome team in those days boasting stars such as Kenny Dalglish, Archie Gemmill, Graeme Souness and Gordon McQueen to name but a few. Playing at Hampden Park had always been an ambition of mine as everyone in the game has heard of the Hampden roar. It certainly didn't disappoint either as the Scots love their football and went mental when we came out. Some aimed a few choice words in my direction but I used to love it when fans had a pop at me, it just made me play even better.

There were, however, to be no heroics on this occasion as I just couldn't get into the game. Chances were few and far between and I hardly touched the ball. When Scotland went a goal up I really couldn't see us getting anything but then in the last minute Willie Donachie attempted a back pass, which he mishit horribly, and it went in. As I was the closest Welsh player to Willie I tried to claim an assist, but no one was having it. In any event, we had now played the two toughest teams in the tournament and hadn't done too badly.

I hoped that we could end on a high by beating Northern Ireland at the Racecourse.

Expectations of a win were high, but Northern Ireland were never going to be a pushover, particularly with players like Martin O'Neill, Sammy McIlroy and Gerry Armstrong in their team. Again there wasn't a lot to choose between us, and the game could have easily gone either way, but we won thanks to a Nick Deacey penalty. It was great to finish with a win, and although my goal-scoring run had ended, I had loved every minute. I was never going to be a first-choice forward for my country, but I hoped I had shown that I was an option.

My next cap for Wales came in 1979 when I was called up to play, in a European Championship qualifier, at the Racecourse, against Turkey. I was named amongst the substitutes, but managed to get on late into the game, by which time Nick Deacey had given us the lead. Nick's goal was enough for us to seal the win, but I think I only touched the ball a few times so it wasn't the most memorable game for me.

Shortly afterwards Mike Smith asked if I would play as an overage player for Wales under-21s against England. I jumped at the chance. If he had asked me to be the kit man for my country I would have done it, because I was happy to represent Wales at any level. Leighton Phillips was also selected as an overage player and Mike told us that he wanted to play us at the back together, as he thought we could be a good partnership for the seniors.

England's under-21s were a formidable outfit back then. Glenn Hoddle, Bryan Robson and Russell Osman were in their team and they would all of course go on to have glittering careers. Even though it was only the under-21s I knew I would still have to be at my best to keep them quiet. The Vetch played host to the game and it felt strange to be cheered rather than booed for once but some Jacks in the crowd still couldn't resist having a go at me. I have never understood why anyone would want to insult a guy who was sweating blood for his, and your, country.

In any event, Leighton and I had played together for Cardiff so we already knew each other's strengths and weaknesses. This meant that we struck up an immediate understanding. On the night we both put in a decent shift and kept that talented England team relatively quiet, but the majestic Glenn Hoddle popped up with a goal to win the game. It is never nice to lose but I was pleased that Leighton and I had done well and hoped that Mike Smith thought the same.

Following Mike's experimentation Leighton and I were both included in his home-international squad for the summer of 1979. He obviously felt that we had done a good job for the under-21s, which was great, and Leighton and I were confident that, if given the chance, we could be a formidable defensive duo for the seniors.

By this stage confidence was high in the Wales squad. Not only had we done reasonably well in the last home-international tournament but we were also top of our European Championship group. Adding to the feel-good factor was that both Cardiff and Swansea were really flying. Richie Morgan had led Cardiff to ninth spot in the second division and John Toshack had completely revolutionised Swansea. Some were even touting them as favourites for promotion to the first division the following season.

Even though Tosh was working wonders in management he still continued to play for both Swansea and Wales and he joined up with us for our first game of the home internationals, against Scotland, at Ninian Park. With Tosh up front Mike Smith came to see me the day before the game and asked if I would be confident man-marking Kenny Dalglish. Kenny was one of the best players in Europe at the time, so it was a daunting prospect, but I told Mike that I would give 100 per cent.

I think this was the first time that Scotland had played in Wales since Joe Jordan's infamous handball, in a World Cup qualifier at Anfield, in 1977. Joe's flapping limb had resulted in the Scots wrongly being awarded a penalty and had ended Wales's World Cup-qualification dream. Obviously feelings were still running high, amongst the fans and players, and as a result Ninian Park was a bear pit. Every time a Scottish player went to take a throw, or a corner, they were pelted with coins and verbally abused. I certainly don't condone that sort of thing, but it made for a very intimidating atmosphere, which we took full advantage of.

Adding to the atmosphere was John Toshack's return to Ninian Park. Tosh was a Cardiff City legend and had been brilliant during his time as a Bluebird. However, now that he was Swansea boss, I don't think some of the fans quite knew how to take to him. One way to get fans on your side is to play out of your skin and Tosh definitely did that as he scored a perfect hat-trick: one with his head, one with his left and one with his right. He was a fantastic player, almost unplayable in the air, but also brilliant with the ball on the floor, and, despite being in the twilight of his career, he showed the fans the full array of his talent that day.

I like to think that I had also shown that I could do a job at the back at this level. Sticking to Kenny Dalglish like glue, I followed him wherever he went and I knew it was vital that I stayed tight to him. If he managed to turn me, or built up pace to run at me, then the odds were that he would leave me for dead. Every time the ball was played to him I either intercepted it or clattered him. Some of my defending was crude, but it did the job as Kenny made no impact and was eventually substituted. When Dalglish left the pitch my afternoon's work wasn't over because public-enemy-number-one, Joe Jordan, then entered the fray. Even though he had robbed Wales of a chance to play at a World Cup I actually felt a bit sorry for him because when he came onto the pitch the place erupted. It was one of the most hostile receptions I have ever heard.

Jordan was a top player, who loved a good scrap with a defender, and we both really went at each other. It was a good tussle, but I always preferred playing against a physical forward, compared to a nippy, skilful one. I knew that I could hold my own when it came to playing against big target men and I like to think that on the day I got the better of Joe. Over the course of ninety minutes I had kept two of British football's best attackers, Kenny Dalglish and Joe Jordan, quiet. It was a great feeling and made me feel that if I was ever given the opportunity to play in the first division I could do a job.

England, at Wembley, were our next opponents and after the job I did on Kenny Dalglish, Mike Smith asked me to man-mark Kevin Keegan. Kevin was the reigning European footballer of the year and at the time was enjoying great success in Germany with Hamburg. It would be another tough assignment but I felt that if I could just stay tight then he would have to be at his best to get the better of me.

On the day I put in one of my best displays in a Wales shirt, and, as my confidence grew, I took my mind off kicking Keegan and tried to play a bit of football. At one point I remember the ball was knocked down the right-hand side of the field and Kevin and I set off to get to it. I had a few yards head start, so I got there first, but as I touched the ball Kevin was already tight behind me. I really don't know what I was thinking but I started to juggle the ball and then flicked it over Kevin's head. The Wales supporters went crazy, it was probably the most skilful thing I had done in my life. Kevin stood rooted to the spot as I ran past him. Doing that kind of thing wasn't natural to me, especially against the European footballer of the year. I think I had a rush of blood after that because whenever the ball came down I didn't calmly control it and pass it to a teammate, I lumped it into row Z.

Having marked Kevin out of the game we emerged with a morale-boosting goalless draw. As a reward for my display I was determined to get Kevin's shirt as a souvenir, and as a scalp. When I asked him for it he laughed and said, 'You may as well have it. You've been tugging at it all afternoon.'

Amazingly, we had the opportunity to win the tournament in our final game against Northern Ireland. It would not, however, be an easy task as the game was at Windsor Park and they also had a chance of winning it. With the stakes high we only managed a draw, which was enough to see Northern Ireland crowned as champions. We were gutted. Our performances throughout the tournament had been top notch, but we weren't rewarded with silverware. It was a bitter pill to swallow.

During the tournament we only conceded one goal, which was incredible. Leighton Phillips and I had played our part, but goalkeeper Dai Davies had been exceptional. Not only was he a top-drawer keeper but he was also a brilliant organiser. He never shut up and would forever be telling you where to position yourself, whether you had a man breathing down your neck and even where you should pass the ball. Sometimes it could get on your nerves, but it really helped. A keeper is one of the few people on the field who can see everything and so his advice is worth listening to. I played with plenty of quiet keepers over my career and I know which type I prefer: a loud, mouthy one like Dai, every day of the week.

After the home internationals my time with the Welsh team wasn't yet over. We still had the small matter of jetting off to Malta to play in a European Championship qualifier. While my football career had to date taken me to less than glamorous destinations, such as Iran and Eastern Europe, I was looking forward to Malta. Although we were obviously going to be playing in a vital game it was a pleasant place to end a long, hard season. All of the boys relished the prospect, apart from the fair-headed lads, like Terry Yorath, who was likely to be burnt to a crisp in the sun.

The trip was everything we expected it to be and more. We were over there for five days and it was lovely to train in the heat and soak up some sun. After training in the morning we were given the afternoon off to sit by the pool or go down to the beach. It was a great few days made even better after a 2–0 win, with goals from Peter Nicholas and Brian Flynn.

With our international games out of the way, and our club season over, everyone was well up for letting their hair down that night. Off we all marched into the town centre and after a few drinks the squad broke off into little groups. There must have been a Welsh player in every bar in town at one point. Mickey Thomas, Joey Jones and I went on a mini bar crawl and in our inebriated state we got a bit rowdy. It was all good natured, and we weren't doing anything wrong, but out of nowhere a police van pulled up alongside us. Before we could move a bunch of cops jumped out, and started shouting at us, but we didn't have a clue what they were saying. We protested our innocence but it cut no ice with the Maltese constabulary and we were marched into the back of the van. I was shitting myself. I had heard all about foreign jails and didn't fancy it one bit. The news of us being locked up would also cause a media storm, which wouldn't do my reputation as a footballer any good. And I knew that my family would be worried when they heard the news.

In vain, the three of us tried to tell the policemen that we were international footballers, in Malta to represent Wales, but they wouldn't listen. Just as I started to panic the van came to an abrupt stop and the back doors opened. I thought, 'this is it, we're in jail, God help me'. The police hurriedly ushered us out, and while I was expecting the worst, they pointed to a bar across the road. Stood outside were the rest of the Wales squad, sinking a few beers. Patting us on the back the police then drove away, leaving us free to join up with the boys. I couldn't believe my luck, one minute I was expecting to spend the night in a cell and the next I was back drinking in a bar. After that close call I was definitely on my best behaviour.

My last game for my country came in a vital European Championship qualifier, in Cologne, against hot favourites West Germany. Following my exploits against Keegan and Dalglish I approached the game with a spring in my step. West Germany may have been one of the best teams in Europe but I felt that I could handle their star players, Karl Heinz Rummenigge and Klaus Fischer. Mike Smith must have felt the same way because he asked me to keep a close eye on Fischer.

It's fair to say that neither I, nor my teammates, covered ourselves in glory that night in Cologne. My cocky swagger was soon made to look foolish as Rummenigge and Fischer tore us apart. Their first-half performance was the best I had ever seen and I just couldn't believe their quality. Fischer was sensational and he scored a hat-trick to help give the Germans a 5–0 lead at half time. The atmosphere in our dressing room at the break was desolate. We had been well and truly shown up.

Mike Smith attempted to rally us but we knew we were no match for stars such as these. They were untouchable. We approached the second half apprehensively, knowing that if we made a mistake we would be punished. Thankfully, the Germans were satisfied with their night's work and took their foot off the gas, which meant we avoided abject humiliation. Completely against the run of play, Alan Curtis managed to score, which meant that we won the second half 1–0, although it wasn't much consolation.

I wanted to get out of Germany as quickly as possible. Trying to compete with stars of that calibre had left me physically and mentally drained. All I wanted to do was sit by myself, have a cold beer and reflect. Unfortunately, on the team coach, an over-enthusiastic journalist sat next to me and decided to ask me a silly question. 'So Phil, how did that go for you?' I looked at him incredulously before picking him up by his collar and throwing him off the bus. 'How did that go for you?' Yeah, it went really well. I enjoyed getting nutmegged countless times in front of thousands of people and watching my country get humiliated. Idiot!

It was a real shame that my international career ended on such a sour note as up until then I had enjoyed every minute. In a strange way I actually count myself lucky that I was able to be on the same pitch with such great players and witness them at their peak, despite sometimes getting the run around. Of course I would have loved to have played more, but I would have been grateful to get a single minute in Welsh colours let alone playing in tournaments and quali-fiers. My time on the international stage provided me with memories that have lasted a lifetime.

Not a day goes by when I don't stop and think of those happy days.

# 14

# A New Decade, A New Start?

Richie Morgan had done so well during his stint as caretaker manager that the club not only gave him the job on a permanent basis, but also continued to back him heavily in the transfer market. Like a kid in a sweetshop he wasted no time in snapping up players. First in was little Billy Ronson, who joined us from Blackpool for a club record £130,000. Billy may have been small in stature, but he had a huge heart and a fighting spirit. On the pitch he would be everywhere, niggling at people, winning the ball and keeping possession, just like Billy Bremner. Off the pitch he was a good-looking guy who obviously fancied himself as a ladies' man but he also couldn't resist biting when a bit of banter flew his way. You could say anything, absolutely anything, and he would bite. I think he had a slight chip on his shoulder because of his size but he was good fun and fitted in with everyone.

With the club splashing the cash on Billy I wasn't surprised when I heard that we had accepted a bid of £120,000 from Birmingham City for Tony Evans. It was a lot of money and I think Richie took the view that Ronnie Moore would settle down that season and start scoring and he could therefore afford to let Evo go. It was a shame as Evo had a great goal-scoring record, but he was from the Midlands, so he was keen to go back home, and the club made a lot of money, so I suppose the move made sense.

Following our exploits in the second half of the previous season, there was a real buzz around the club during the summer of 1979.

Fans, players, management and directors all believed that we could finally mount a serious promotion push. We were solid at the back, with Ron Healey in goal and Linden Jones, Dave Roberts, Colin Sullivan and me in defence. Creativity, graft and goals were provided in midfield by John Buchanan, Alan Campbell, Billy Ronson and Ray Bishop. In attack we had Gary Stevens, who had proved he could score goals at this level, and Ronnie Moore, who had struggled to settle, but had shown earlier in his career that he knew where the back of the net was. On top of all that we had a well-respected management team of Richie, Doug and Brian and a great chairman in Bob Grogan. Everything was in place for us to do well.

As is always the case when expectation levels are high things tend not to go so well and we started the season disastrously, losing 4–1 at Notts County. With ten minutes to go the score had actually been 1–1, and we had played well, but then we collapsed. It was very disappointing but I put it down as just one of those days and wasn't too disheartened.

Thankfully, we soon started to display our form from the previous season, especially Gary Stevens, who scored in five consecutive games and helped us to wins over QPR, Wrexham and Shrewsbury, as well as a draw at Watford. However, the one game that Gary scored in, but that we lost in this spell, came against Tony Evans's Birmingham City, at Ninian Park. Typically, Evo scored twice for them that day but he still received applause from our fans as he left the pitch. No doubt everyone affectionately recalled his fantastic partnership with Adrian Alston from just a few years before.

While Gary was scoring for fun Ronnie Moore couldn't buy a goal. It took until the twelfth game of the season for him to get off the mark and yet again his finishing in some games had been less than clinical. Richie knew that he needed to bring someone in to help shoulder the goal-scoring burden so he started looking for strikers. Knowing that we had a bit of money to spend I was hopeful that we could sign a proven forward but it didn't turn out that way. Completely out of the blue, Wayne Hughes joined us for £70,000 from Tulsa Roughnecks. It is fair to say that I was underwhelmed.

Not only could I not understand why we had signed a player like Wayne but the fee was also astronomical for someone of his ability.

Wayne was originally from Port Talbot, a lovely lad who I don't have a bad word for. Getting a move back to Cardiff was a dream come true for him and I don't blame him for jumping at the chance. However, he just wasn't up to it at this level. It wasn't that he was a bad player but he hadn't really set the world alight in the US and for the money we had paid I was sure there were far more talented players available. It was a deal that never sat well with me. I've always been suspicious that someone's pockets must have been lined somewhere along the way as it just didn't make sense. Plenty of the boys raised their eyebrows.

Another player that Richie brought in was goalkeeper Peter Grotier, from Lincoln City. Ron Healey had been in good form, but had suffered a few injuries so I think Richie just wanted Grots to come in as back up. What a lad Grots was, he loved playing practical jokes and would have us all in stitches. One of my favourite tales about Grots concerns Paul Giles, or 'Possum' as he was known in the dressing room. He hated being called Possum back then, and he hates it even more now, but I'm sorry Gilo, the name has stuck. Anyway, Possum was one of the more gullible guys at the club. If you told him anything he would take it as gospel so he was always a good target or a wind up. Before training one day the boys told Possum that Grots was gay and looking for a boyfriend. Possum wouldn't have it.

'Grots, gay? No chance,' he said.

Tightening the screw I told him, 'Haven't you noticed yet, Grots is as camp as Christmas.' He still wasn't convinced but he started to look at Grots in a funny way.

After training, as we were getting changed, I decided to keep the gag going. I whispered to Possum.

'You better watch yourself mate. When we were doing stretches Grots told me that he thinks you have a nice ass.'

'Fuck off Joey, no he never,' Possum snapped back.

'He did mate, I'm serious. I think he quite fancies you,' I replied.

Poor Possum's face was a picture. He didn't know what to do.

'Look,' I said, trying to keep a straight face, 'it's obvious there's a bit of sexual tension between you. It would probably be for the best for both of you if you got it out of the way.'

Possum wasn't amused. He fired a few choice expletives my way and then went for a shower.

When Possum eventually came out the boys were waiting for him. Before he could run we grabbed him and held him down on the physio's table. It makes me laugh even thinking about it now because he didn't have a clue what was going on and he was really panicking. Suddenly Grots entered the room, licking his lips, and wearing just a towel round his waist. Mincing up to the table he said in his campest voice, 'I really fancy you Paul. I think you're gorgeous.' Possum was shitting himself. I had to bite my tongue as I was close to hysterics. Grots seductively dropped his towel, leaving him starkers, and moved towards Possum as if he was going to kiss him. I swear Possum had tears in his eyes. I couldn't hold it any longer. I dropped to the floor and pissed myself laughing.

Possum may not have seen the funny side, but stupid things like that build up the camaraderie in a dressing room. Everyone would get picked on, Billy for being so small, Gary for his height and so on and so on. No one got away with anything and I really think that keeps a squad level headed and brings everyone closer together.

Entering November we were all guns blazing as we continued our decent run with wins over Luton, Burnley and Notts County. While we had also lost a few we were still in the top half of the table and a promotion push was very much on the cards. But then, suddenly, we came a cropper as we lost to Sunderland, Preston and Birmingham and dropped down the table. Matters weren't helped when we lost to high-flying Swansea, on New Year's Day, at the Vetch. What made things even worse was that they scored the winner in the last minute, which was a real kick in the teeth.

Shortly afterwards we lost another Welsh derby, against Newport County, in the Welsh Cup. Newport were a decent team then and they boasted a great forward line in John Aldridge and Tommy Tynan, who both happened to score against us that day. In previous games against Newport I had had a few run-ins with John. He wasn't very big but he certainly put himself about and we both had little niggles at each other. During a league game, as a corner was being floated into our penalty area, I took a sore one from John in an off-the-ball incident, which left me with a broken jaw. He will no doubt claim it was wholly accidental but it didn't look or feel that way to me. From that day on I made sure his name was at the top of the list in my little black book.

In our next game with them the mere sight of John was like a red rag to a bull. I was desperate to leave my mark on him and I think he realised how I felt as he did everything he could to stay away from me. Late in the game I got the chance I had been waiting for. John was running with the ball, but it got away from him slightly, and, as he tried to get it back under control, he didn't see me charging towards him. As he reached the ball I lunged towards him, both feet off the ground, and planted them right in his groin. On impact he squealed and collapsed on the floor in agony. As the ref came charging over I held up my hands, claiming it was an accident. Astonishingly, I don't even think I got a booking, but the crowd at Somerton Park certainly let me know what they thought of the tackle. After a long time receiving treatment John somehow managed to play on, but it was obvious that he was hurt, and he didn't do anything for the rest of the game.

Satisfied with my day's work I was enjoying a pint in the player's bar when I saw John approach me. I was certain he was looking for more so I clenched my fist in readiness. He then surprised me when he held out his hand, laughed, and said 'I had been expecting that, and I deserved it. What are you drinking?' We had a good laugh about it and considered the matter closed.

That's what football was like back then. The players sorted out their problems like men and the refs let us get on with it. You would have to do something horrific to get sent off. There was no diving or any of that nonsense; it was just eleven men against eleven men, going at it hammer and tongs. Obviously the game has improved beyond all recognition now – and I love seeing players like Ronaldo and Messi show off their skills – but the edge has disappeared. Tackling is an art but all the rules and regulations regarding what you can and can't do have made the hard men of the game an endangered species. If you think about it, how many players in the modern game can really be described as hard men? I can only think of a handful, if that.

I suppose during my time at Cardiff City I was seen as the team's enforcer. Not only did I have to take care of myself, but I also had to dish it out if one of our flair players was getting some bother. Once when we played against Leicester City, Gary Stevens was getting lumps kicked out of him. After a tussle the player in question kicked Gary and sent him sprawling to the floor. I strode over, turned the

Leicester player round, so that his back was facing me, and said, 'I've got your number now mate. Watch yourself.' The Leicester player told me where to go, but minutes later his game was over when I smacked him off the ball. Without having to worry about this bloke smashing him, Gary Stevens later went on to score the winner. My job was done.

Unfortunately, I didn't always get away with such behaviour. When we played Shrewsbury at Ninian Park I knew right from the start that I had to intimidate one of their players. I can't recall his name now, but he made them tick and if we had let him play he would have run the game. Right from kickoff I followed him wherever he went and proceeded to bombard him with abuse and digs. In the third minute I gave him a kick down his ankle, but the ref saw it out of the corner of his eye and I was given my marching orders. I got away with plenty during my career but if I was playing today I would probably be on an FA disciplinary charge every week.

Following our Welsh Cup dismissal, at the hands of Newport, we continued to struggle in the league. No one was playing particularly well, me included, and we were in desperate need of inspiration. It came from an unlikely source. In the next game we were seeing out a drab 0–0 draw with Wrexham, at Ninian Park, when the much maligned Ronnie Moore struck the winner. It was only his second goal in twenty-five games, yet it couldn't have come at a better time as it helped stop the rot. Ronnie was so low on confidence that he had even started to carry around his house number, as a good-luck charm, on match days. God knows why he did that but he was obviously grasping at straws, trying anything that he could to discover his scoring touch.

Unbelievably, Ronnie's superstitious ploy seemed to work. In the next game, against Shrewsbury, he scored a last-minute winner. Everyone thought that, finally, Ronnie had found his goal-scoring boots, and just at the right time too. Gary Stevens's goals had dried up, and Wayne Hughes had only scored once since his arrival, so we were in desperate need of someone, anyone, to start hitting the back of the net. Unfortunately, it was not to be and his goal against Shrewsbury turned out to be his last in a City shirt.

Sandwiched between the games against Wrexham and Shrewsbury was the little matter of facing Arsenal in the third round of the FA

Cup at Ninian Park. It was a fantastic draw for the club; not only an opportunity to test ourselves against one of the best teams in the country, but also a huge financial boost. In front of 22,000 fans we did ourselves proud. Despite being under the cosh for most of the game, we defended resolutely and earned a goalless draw and a money-spinning replay at Highbury. Winning in north London was always going to be a big ask but, amazingly, we went ahead after Buchy slotted home a penalty. Just as we were dreaming of a giant-killing act Alan Sunderland notched two goals for them and they ran out 2–1 winners. It was disappointing, but playing so well against a top team had done our confidence no harm.

Following the games against Arsenal we then won our third league game on the trot, against Watford. Once again we needed a last-minute winner to get the two points and this time it came courtesy of John Lewis. Back in the top half of the table we at least looked safe, but we couldn't quite build the momentum required to get in the promotion spots as we won a few, drew a few and lost a few.

One game that did prove to be memorable came in the Welsh derby, at the Vetch, on Easter Monday. For many of the lads it was the first time they had played there in Cardiff colours, and I think it took a few of them by surprise. Billy Ronson had grown up in the north-west, a part of the world that has plenty of derbies, but even he was shocked at the ferocity surrounding this game. The fans wanted our heads on sticks and in a ramshackle stadium like the Vetch, where the crowd could almost touch you, it was a frightening experience.

Swansea were still in the hunt for promotion, and we were desperate to dent their chances, but it was always going to be difficult because they were flying. Not only were we playing for points, but we were also playing for pride as neither club had ever done the double over the other in a single season. Ripping up the script we avenged our heartbreaking defeat from New Year's Day with Billy Ronson striking a last-minute winner. Little Billy went berserk when he scored. We all tried to get to him, but he just kept running until he was celebrating in front of the delirious away end.

With little to play for, due to avoiding both promotion and relegation, the season petered out. The previous season we had of course prevented Sunderland from going up, thanks to a famous win at Roker Park, which had delighted Bob Grogan and Jack Leonard. As luck would have it we had another opportunity to stop them in their tracks, on the last day of the season, at Ninian Park. Nothing would have pleased our Geordie chairman more if we had managed to do it again but Sunderland were a good team and only needed a point to go up. We played very well but the Wearsiders got the point they came for. While we finished the season in fifteenth place the Black Cats went up to the first division.

It goes without saying that Bob and Jack weren't too pleased, but although I would have rather won the game, I was happy to see Sunderland go up. A lot of my wife's family lived in the north-east, and were mad Sunderland fans, so I always had a soft spot for them. For some reason a lot of the Cardiff boys were also good mates with their players. I remember that we used to share cup-final tickets with each other and they were always good company in the players' bar after the game.

Although we had come nowhere near a challenge for promotion we had at least avoided a relegation scrap and I was still confident that this squad had what it took if we could recruit just one or two new faces in the summer. Sadly, my confidence was misplaced.

# 15

# Ten Years and Counting

Remarkably, the 1980/81 season was my testimonial year at Cardiff City. I had been at the club for a decade but it still only seemed like yesterday that I was trying to earn a professional contract from Jimmy Scoular. The years had flown by and now the only person who was still at the club with me was Harry Parsons. My time at Ninian Park had certainly been a rollercoaster. One year we would be relegated, the next promoted. Sometimes we would be broke, and worried whether the club could pay our wages, then we would be flush, building a new stand and smashing our transfer record. It was far from dull and through the ups and down I had enjoyed every minute.

Bob Grogan was fantastic. He not only awarded me a testimonial game, against Stoke City, but he also said that if less than ten thousand people turned up the club would pay me the difference. It was a lovely gesture and I really appreciated it. We weren't on big money in those days and every penny helped.

Stoke City were a real glamour team back then. Not only were they a first-division side, who could play some scintillating football, but they also boasted top players such as Sammy McIlroy, Mark Chamberlain and my old Wales pal, Mickey Thomas. There was no doubt that they would add some real stardust to the occasion. To add further star quality I also asked if my Wales teammate, Peter Nicholas, of Arsenal, could guest for the Cardiff team, a request that was happily granted.

The Cardiff fans were always great to me, but even though it was my testimonial, and they would be treated to the sight of some of the best players in the country, I wondered how many would turn up. I needn't have worried. Well over ten thousand fans flocked to Ninian Park, an attendance which turned out to be the second highest of the season. It just backed up what I already knew – Cardiff City have the best supporters in sport!

I have to admit that I hadn't really prepared myself for the emotion of the night. In my eyes it was going to be just another game of football, perhaps marked by a souvenir of some kind, but the outpouring of tributes really caught me off guard, and brought tears to my eyes. Before the game, as I sat in the changing room exchanging banter with the boys, I flicked through the souvenir programme. When I read some of the things that were said about me, by people I respected, I suddenly found my lower lip quivering. Mike England, a man I had always idolised, said that I was 'a manager's dream,' while my old Wales teammate, Terry Yorath chipped in with, 'I can sum up Phil Dwyer in one sentence: the kind of player you love to have in your side . . . and hate to play against. Off the pitch Phil is also one of the nicest men I know. Quiet, kind and with a sharp sense of humour.'

Yet amidst all the praise I was brought down to earth by my wife, Ann, who revealed that decorating wasn't one of my strong points as, 'he usually ends up leaving one window unpainted,' while Mike England put paid to my singing career, 'I can think of just one flaw in his character. For reasons beyond my comprehension, Phil fancies his chances as a singer . . . Joe, Joe please don't do it!' Sorry Mike, but my singing days are still far from over!

Supporters, Ianto Ball, Alwyn Evans, David Roberts and Mike Davies also helped to mark the occasion by presenting me with the following poem:

*A poem for Phil Dwyer,*
*Or Joe as he is often called,*
*On quiet nights at Ninian,*
*At many players he has bawled.*

*Get there, go here,*
*Get back into space,*
*Just waiting for Tarki Micallef,*
*To say 'Shuddupa your face'.*

*But Joe is strong and sturdy,*
*Built from mountain rock,*
*He can head a ball from Ninian Park,*
*Down to Cardiff dock.*

*Whilst playing at number six,*
*Any player he cannot outjump,*
*When up to his old tricks,*
*There is always room for a thump.*

*He has played some games for Wales,*
*In fact, quite a few times,*
*Of course playing against England,*
*Can be quite a bind.*

*With players like Kevin Keegan,*
*Poncing around the field,*
*Joe just stands and growls,*
*Until they stop and yield.*

*Now for the City,*
*He has scored a few good goals,*
*Takes the odd risk and gamble,*
*Different sort to Stan Bowles.*
*When asked, 'Who are your favourite players,*
*If they are not in heaven,'*
*He will say, 'There are ten I know at Cardiff,*
*Oh, and me that makes my eleven.'*

*He is quite a fun character,*
*In the air, or on his feet,*
*Even when out shopping,*
*In the local high street.*

*Crack a joke, tell a tale,*
*Or even take the mick,*
*Of some big useless forward,*
*Who is tall, skinny and thick.*

*Whilst stood next to Toshack,*
*In Cologne, it was a joy to see,*
*That all the Welsh support,*
*Came from Cardiff City.*

*So make his testimonial,*
*A great night for him,*
*And while you're at the bar Joe,*
*Mine's a double gin.*

I was touched that the fans had spent time writing such a lovely poem about me and to this day I have it on display in my house.

To be completely honest, I was so taken back by all the nice things people were saying, and by the breathtaking reception the fans gave me, that I can't recall much about the game. Everything was a blur, and I couldn't concentrate on playing, as I was too busy trying to take it all in. It didn't seem real that a first-division team, and thousands of fans, had come down to Ninian Park just for me. Even now, just thinking about it gets me emotional.

For weeks after the game I continued to be touched by the trouble the fans took to let me know what they thought of me. I received countless letters from supporters, who not only expressed their admiration for me, but also enclosed money for my testimonial fund. What amazing people! I treasure those letters and the following one has always been special to me.

*Dear Mr Grogan,*

*I get to see nearly all City's games home and away over a season. However, I was unable to swap shifts last Tuesday and was forced to miss Phil Dwyer's testimonial match. This was a big disappointment as it has been a great pleasure to watch Joe play over the years. He epitomised the never say die spirit of Cardiff City so often seen in recent years and if he were not playing I'm pretty sure he would be among those watching from the terraces. Please pass on my good wishes for the future to Phil.*

*I enclose gate money, and a little more, because I was present in mind on Tuesday, if not in person, and feel happy to contribute to the testimonial of such a marvellous City player.*

*Yours in sport,*

*Robert G Hellier*

If you are reading this Mr Hellier, God bless you!

Putting my testimonial to one side there continued to be changes at the club in an attempt to push us forward. As Bob Grogan and Jack Leonard still operated primarily from the north-east they felt that they needed someone to be based full time in Cardiff to help them run the club. For that reason Ron Jones was hired that summer to act as the club's general manager. In his heyday Ron had been a great athlete, who had represented Britain at the Olympics, and even though he was meant to be looking after the administrative side he started taking us for sprinting drills. Oblivious to our lack of interest he tried to show us the correct technique for running but in the early 1980s training of that sort was unheard of for footballers and we were all very sceptical. Most top clubs probably do things like this on a regular basis now, and it is no doubt very useful, but back then everyone thought it was strange and it didn't last very long. Looking back I wish I had listened, I probably could have learnt a thing or two.

It came as no surprise when Ronnie Moore finally left the club that summer, after spending eighteen months with us and scoring a grand total of six goals. Not quite the return you are hoping for from a £100,000 striker. Incredibly, Rotherham were quite happy to pay us that same figure for his services and I don't think the club could believe its luck. Despite his profligacy in front of goal down here I was still confident that he could do well elsewhere and that proved to be the case. He went on to score a hatful of goals for Rotherham and has of course had great success as their manager in recent years. I still speak to Ronnie from time to time and he is someone I have a lot of time for. Plenty of players would have crumbled under the pressure he was subjected to at Cardiff but he was so good natured and determined that we had nothing but respect for the guy.

In Ronnie's place came Peter Kitchen from Fulham. Kitch was a typical goal scorer who would get most of his goals in the penalty area. He was a real fox in the box. Off the ball he may not have done the same amount of work as Ronnie but he was bought to score goals and as long as he did that no one would care. Paul Maddy also looked set to play a big part in the forthcoming season. He was one of the star players from our youth system and he had fantastic technique. As he was still so young he needed a bit more meat on him but everyone at the club thought he could go on and be a big player for us.

Leaving the club that summer was Alan Campbell, who signed for Carlisle. AC was an excellent player, who had done well during his time as a Bluebird, and I was a little surprised that we allowed him to leave. Yes, he was getting on and his legs had started to go, but he could read the game as well as anyone and was one of the few we had who could keep hold of the ball. Although losing AC was surprising I was staggered when I heard that both Doug Livermore and Brian Harris had been let go. I think it was on financial grounds, but I thought it was a crazy decision. Richie had done well, but he was still a young manager, and Doug and Brian had played a huge part in his success. Without the two of them I started to wonder whether we would be going backwards again.

With so much upheaval at the club we had an inconsistent start to the season. It seemed that we would win, lose, win, lose, win, lose. My own form was, however, decent and I even managed to score against both Leyton Orient and Notts County. Gary Stevens was also playing well, and managing to hit the target for us on a regular basis, but at one point it looked as if the curse of Ronnie Moore was striking Peter Kitchen as he missed a hatful of chances in the first few games. Once he hit his first City goal against Newcastle United, in our fifth game of the season, he thankfully went from strength to strength.

During the first few weeks of the season we progressed nicely in the League Cup by beating Torquay United and then Chelsea. This meant that in the third round we had to face Burnley at Turf Moor. During the course of my career I had to witness some truly inept refereeing displays but the ref that night was abysmal. As the game entered the fourth minute of injury time we were losing 2–1, but John

Lewis equalised at the death to set up a replay at Ninian Park. During the game there had been a couple of substitutions, and one or two minor injuries, but nothing to suggest that there were any more than four minutes of injury time. Everyone fully expected the final whistle to blow but the ref, incredibly, let the game continue.

We were all bemused and kept shouting, 'Come on ref. That has to be time,' but he ignored us. Then in the seventh minute of injury time, and to our intense fury, Burnley scored. To this day I haven't got a clue where the added time came from and we were so incensed that we surrounded the referee and vented our spleen at him. What rubbed even more salt into the wound was that when we kicked off he immediately blew the final whistle and ran straight off the pitch. Richie was apoplectic and chased him down the tunnel, determined to find out where all that extra time had come from, but the ref refused to speak to him. Understandably, Richie blew his top. It was probably the angriest I ever saw him. There was nothing we could do about it but the sense of injustice we felt was considerable. It was one of the most outrageous things I witnessed during my time in football.

Following the League Cup debacle our form really began to slide. Gary Stevens stopped scoring, and while Kitch was getting a few, at one stage we still only scored four goals in eight games. Defensively, we weren't doing too badly but if you are not scoring goals it makes it impossible to win games. As a result, we went through November drawing six consecutive matches.

Swansea, at Ninian Park, were our opponents for one of those draws and while derby games are always memorable this clash has taken on legendary status. Tosh had really got Swansea playing, and they were near the top of the table, blowing teams away at will. That day they were superb and well in control, leading 3–1, with just minutes remaining. Richie had subbed me at this point, and had brought on an attacker, so I sat in the dugout feeling sick to my stomach at the sight of the Swans tearing us apart. Even some of the crowd had started to give up and hordes of people left the Bob Bank and made their way down Sloper Road.

Then, against the run of play, Kitch scored what appeared to be a consolation goal as the game went into the ninetieth minute. Deep into injury time we won a free kick, about forty-five yards from the

Swansea goal. Buchy put the ball down and then took a long run up, suggesting he was going to have a crack. He had a hell of a shot on him but even I was dubious as to whether he would have much joy from that distance. I remember that as Buchy lined up to have a go Tosh shouted at his players, 'Let him shoot, he'll never score from there.' As Buchy sprinted forward the ball was tapped to the side, ready for him to smash. He caught the ball sweetly and as it hurtled towards the goal I stood up at the back of the dugout to get a better view. Like an Exocet missile the ball gathered pace and it slammed into the top corner, almost taking the net off. When it went in I jumped up and banged my head against the dugout roof. Bedlam broke out in the stadium. The Cardiff fans who had been on their way out of the ground had stayed to watch Buchy's free kick and they were going berserk. You could hear the cheers going all the way down Sloper Road. It felt as if we had won a cup final and I can honestly say it is the best goal I have ever seen. Of course the fact that it came against our greatest rivals, and gave us an unlikely draw, made it even better.

In the dressing room after the game we were buzzing and Richie told us we could build our season on a comeback like that. If only. We went on to lose four straight games, were knocked out of the FA Cup by Leicester and slumped towards the relegation zone.

The atmosphere within the squad became more and more fraught as we continued to slide. Things came to a head when John Lewis and Ray Bishop had a punch up in a nightclub. I wasn't there but I was shocked when I heard that those two had been fighting. They were good mates, always messing around, and there were plenty of others I would have thought would have had a ruck before them. Bish was so small he didn't look like he could hurt a fly, but he must have really caught John, who was in a right state. I'm told that he was lucky not to lose the sight in one eye. I can't remember why the fight started, but I know Bish was distraught. Despite his apologies he was soon sent packing to Newport, which was a shame as he was a good player who popped up with a few goals.

As we continued to plummet down the table it really highlighted to me just what a foolish decision it had been to get rid of Doug Livermore and Brian Harris. Not only were they good coaches, who knew the game inside out, but they also lightened the atmosphere with their humour. Without them we were rudderless, and petty squabbles and fights in training were reflected in our performances, as we continued to lose. Peter Kitchen's goals were just about the only thing keeping us in with a chance of avoiding relegation. Entering the final stretch we were in and out of the drop zone and I knew it was going to be touch and go whether we stayed up. We had two home games to finish off the season but both were against tough opposition, Derby and West Ham. Staying up was by no means certain.

We enjoyed doing things the hard way and the game with Derby ended goalless, which meant that we needed to avoid defeat to West Ham, on the last day of the season, to be certain of avoiding the drop. The game was very tense and there wasn't a real opening for either team during the entire ninety minutes. As long as we didn't lose we knew that we were safe so we weren't particularly adventurous, relying instead on a stout defensive performance to see us through. Despite it being a dull and uninspiring game, we again drew 0–0 and managed to avoid relegation on goal difference.

The season hadn't panned out in the way I expected. I knew that the club was now in a precarious situation. If we added new players in the summer, and sorted out the backroom staff, we could still be promotion contenders. However, if we failed to address those issues then there was no doubt in my mind that relegation could be on the cards and that would spell disaster.

# 16

# The Blue Dragons

It was abundantly clear that money was going to be tight at the club in the summer of 1981. Losing Doug Livermore and Brian Harris on financial grounds during the previous campaign had shown that the club was now cutting its cloth according to its means. While I didn't expect a flurry of new signings I did hope that, at the very least, we would address the coaching situation. Since Doug and Brian's departure it was obvious to all and sundry that we weren't the same team. Regrettably, the board had other ideas and instead of putting money into the football club they came up with one of the most ridiculous ideas I had ever heard. They set up a rugby-league club!

The club in question was named the Cardiff Blue Dragons and they would play at Ninian Park, which certainly wouldn't help the pitch. The players were stunned when the news broke. The club was struggling to support a football team so how on earth was it also going to be able to fund a professional rugby-league team as well? It didn't make sense. Obviously, someone on the board thought that it could be another revenue stream. They hoped that in time the Dragons could support themselves and that if successful some of that money would filter down to the football club. That to me was wishful thinking.

I have always enjoyed the rugby, particularly in the Seventies when the Wales national side was unbeatable, but I couldn't see this new venture paying off. Unsurprisingly, Cardiff City supporters were up in arms. We had narrowly avoided relegation the previous season, and they expected us to bring in some new blood, but now that wasn't going to be possible. In my eyes it was professional suicide.

While a lack of funds for new coaching staff and players was going to make life difficult, the board, in its wisdom, also decided to scrap our reserve team, as well as our Welsh League side. This really baffled me and I knew that it would severely affect our performances on the pitch. How were players coming back from injury, or those who couldn't get into the first team, going to keep fit and sharp? You can train all you like but there is no substitute for games. Although the standard of the Welsh League, and the Combination, was nowhere near the Football League it was still decent and certainly far superior to training.

To me the board was doing everything in its power to ruin our chances for the season ahead. They did however finally see sense when it came to the coaching situation as Richie was allowed to replace Doug and Brian. Having seen the benefits of former players coming back in a coaching capacity, Richie brought in former goalkeeper, Fred Davies, as well as Bobby Woodruff. Colin Prophet also joined the backroom staff and while all three made an immediate impact on the training ground they had a tough act to follow in Brian and Doug.

One of the few players who did join us that summer was Paul Sugrue, who came in on a free transfer from Manchester City. Suggy was a hell of a character and he had the skill to match his banter. He was like a radio, just non-stop chatter, and was always thinking up pranks and gags. Sometimes he would go too far, and someone would give him a slap, but he never meant any harm and he certainly brightened up the place. Despite all the problems that summer we actually went through pre-season unbeaten and looked decent, with local boy Tarki Micallef and Kitch looking especially sharp. To this day I still blame Tarki for the hole in the ozone layer. He had a bouffant hairdo and would spend hours in front of the mirror, covering every strand with hairspray. Everywhere he went he would carry a little can of spray and he would be constantly fiddling with his barnet.

Our pre-season form made me think that I had been too harsh in my assessment of the team, and the board, and that things just might turn out for the best. If only. We started as we meant to go on and within six minutes of our first league game of the season we were 2–0 down to Oldham. It certainly looked as if we were going to be on the end of a humiliating score line, but Gary Stevens got one back and then yours truly grabbed the equaliser. We were relieved. No one likes to lose on the opening day and a comeback like that felt like a win. We didn't have an awful lot of flair in our team but I hoped that our fighting spirit would see us through.

The point we earned at Oldham was, however, the only one that we got in our first four games as we proceeded to lose to Chelsea, Rotherham and Blackburn. Who should be the match winner in the Rotherham game, but the much maligned Ronnie Moore? It was so typical. He couldn't hit a cow's ass with a banjo when he was with us, but now he was scoring for fun. While I hated to lose I was glad that Ronnie was doing well. It is incredible how a player can look so out of place at one club but elsewhere perform like a world beater.

With our form continuing to be poor Richie pulled off a master stroke when he signed defender Gary Bennett from Manchester City. As soon as Gary joined us for training it was clear that he was going to be too good for this level. He was quick, athletic, could read the game, had great technique and could put himself about. I felt that together we had the makings of a decent centre-back partnership; I could add graft and grit to his flair and pace. Gary was one of the flashest players I came across in my time at Cardiff. Some of his gear was horrendous. He loved brightly coloured clothes and whenever he came into a room I would shield my eyes with my hands and say, 'Bloody hell Benno, turn the lights off.' He was a great lad though, nothing bothered him and he took everything in his stride.

If we were going to get out of our slump it was clear that we needed additional reinforcements so Richie brought back Peter Sayer, on a month's loan, from Brighton. Getting a player of Leo's ability, even if it was just for a month, was a no brainer. He knew the club inside out so he could settle easily and hit the ground running.

With Gary and Leo in the team we beat Luton and Leo even managed to get on the score sheet. Richie's business in the transfer market looked inspired. Seeing the benefits that new players brought to the squad the board again backed Richie's judgement by somehow raising £120,000 to sign Gary Bennett's brother, Dave, also from Man

City. I haven't got a clue where we found the money, but thank God we did, as Dave was a revelation on the wing. He had pace to burn, and knew every trick and flick in the book, but he also had an eye for goal and could deliver a great cross. It had been a long time since we had a player in Dave's class and we were told to get the ball to him at every opportunity. The fans loved him; he was electric and had them on the edge of their seats.

We all loved Benno as a bloke as well. He was a top lad who had us in tears with his stories. While his brother, Gary, was chilled and laid back Benno was competing with Suggy to be crowned the loudest player at the club. Even his laugh was infectious. Benno made his debut in a 1–0 win at Barnsley and with Gary and Leo also in the side we looked as if we were ready to put our poor start to the season behind us and begin looking up the table. However, a reality check arrived in our next game against Newcastle, who hammered us 4–0 at home, a result that saw us get booed off the pitch.

Matters weren't helped when the board decided to sell Billy Ronson and John Buchanan to recoup the money they spent had on Benno. I thought the Benno money had been too good to be true. Both Ronson and Buchanan were key men, and while having Benno and Gary was great, we knew that we couldn't afford to lose any class players. It wasn't as if Benno and Gary had taken Billy and Buchy's places and that they were now surplus to requirements. We had strengthened our defence and right wing but had then decimated the spine of our team by flogging two of our best centre midfielders.

Our home form had been so poor in 1981 that after defeating Newcastle, on 25 February, we didn't win again until 17 October, during the following season, when we beat Bolton 2–1, courtesy of Benno, who scored the winner. Ninian Park had always been a fortress, but for whatever reason we just couldn't buy a win there during that spell. No one likes paying money to watch their team when they are on such a dire run, and as a result only 3,879 turned up for the Bolton game. We were in the equivalent of the Championship and these days it is considered a poor crowd if we get less than twenty thousand turning up.

With just a few thousand fans rattling around a ground like Ninian Park it is very difficult to generate an atmosphere. It goes without saying that players should always be pumped up, but the crowd's support, and the noise they generate, is a big help. Those who did turn up sang and cheered as best they could, but I have to admit that it was soul destroying playing in front of a near-empty stadium. Sometimes I wondered whether we would ever again see the glory days, with the ground close to bursting, as the likes of the mighty Real Madrid came to town.

We may have thought that our crowds were poor, but the rugby-league team were faring even worse. Their gates hovered around the thousand mark and it was a struggle to keep them afloat. It was amazing that in a city renowned for its sporting success, the rugby league and football sides couldn't get a decent crowd even when the combined attendances were added up.

Despite the doom and gloom we followed up our win over Bolton with victories over Norwich and Wrexham and sat comfortably in ninth place. I just wished the club hadn't sacked Doug and Brian, had stayed clear of setting up a rugby team and had kept Billy and Buchy. If they had got those three decisions right we would have had a good shot at winning the title, of that I am certain. Richie had worked wonders in the circumstances and deserved the plaudits. Not everyone, however, felt the same.

In one of the most baffling decisions I ever came across in my time in football, Richie Morgan was asked to step down as manager and to move into an administrative position. I was astonished. None of the players could understand it but we assumed the club had a big name ready to take the reins. That could be the only explanation for such a rash move. We had been on a good run, Richie had signed players of exceptional ability in Gary and Dave Bennett, and we were in ninth place. Why get rid of him?

When we heard that the club had appointed Graham Williams as the new manager, it is fair to say that we were all disappointed. Graham had a decent career as a player – turning out for West Brom and Wales – but he had no managerial experience. It's not as if he had even earned a reputation as a good coach because since retiring from the game he had been running a health-food shop in Weymouth. It didn't add up. As players we had to grin and bear it, but we were baffled. I thought that Graham may have convinced the board he had a master plan to take the club forward, but he hardly changed a thing. He was a decent, mild-mannered bloke, whom everyone seemed to like, but it was clear from the start that he wasn't any better than Richie.

Initially, results were good as we drew at Watford, and then beat Leicester and Derby. We were, however, on a good run of form before Graham's arrival and whenever a new manager comes in players subconsciously give that little bit more as they know they are fighting for their place. Unfortunately, after we beat Derby on the fourth of December we didn't win another game until the twentieth of March and in consequence found ourselves deep in relegation trouble. From being genuine promotion candidates we were now struggling to survive.

With no light at the end of a very dark tunnel, we were given a rare day out in January to enjoy ourselves, in the form of an FA Cup tie, at Maine Road, against Manchester City. No one was looking forward to this game more than Gary and Dave Bennett, who, of course, we had bought from City. Even though we lost the game 3–1, with young Paul Maddy scoring a goal he would never forget, Maine Road was a great ground to play at and our fans enjoyed every minute. We didn't disgrace ourselves and it was nice to have a brief distraction from our travails in the second division.

After Maine Road our league form continued to be poor which was bad news for the manager. He was sacked on 3 March, and even though Richie was blameless for this sequence of results, he also left the club. No one was surprised to see Graham go. It was clear that if a change wasn't made we had no hope of staying up. Though it wasn't too late to save ourselves we knew it would take a monumental effort. If the club wanted to make a fight of it my view was that they had to bring in an experienced man to lead us out of trouble. Fortunately, the board pulled off a masterstroke by appointing Len Ashurst. Len may have been recently sacked by Newport, but he had done a great job for them, on a shoestring, over a number of years. He had also done well at Hartlepool, Gillingham and Sheffield Wednesday. Len not only had good managerial experience but he was also settled in south Wales so he could get straight down to work with no distractions. Under the circumstances, I thought it was a good move for all concerned.

Rolling up his sleeves Len threw himself into the job. He attended every training session and made it clear that no one was going to slack on his watch. We were also delighted that he wanted us to play football and so a lot of our drills focused on keeping possession. There was also a lot of emphasis put on attack; Len was going to go for broke in an attempt to win games.

The new man's first game in charge was against Cambridge United at Ninian Park. Only three thousand showed up, which only goes to show just how underwhelmed the supporters were by this stage, but those who did come were rewarded with the best game of the season as we won 5–4. Len's adventurous approach had worked wonders, although it has to be said that it left us open at the back. The new attacking philosophy was a risky move, but with the club still in the relegation zone, and just a handful of games remaining, it was clear that we couldn't rely on trying to nick games by defending. We had to blow teams away.

Having assessed the squad Len advised the board that if we were to have any chance of staying up we needed new blood. Staring relegation in the face the board allowed him to sign Andy Dibble, a goalkeeper, Andy Polycarpou, an attack-minded midfielder and Jimmy Mullen and Mick Henderson, two experienced defenders. They were all good acquisitions and played their part in our attempt to beat the drop.

Games came thick and fast during the final few weeks and our new manager, and his signings, made an impact as we won three consecutive home games, against Grimsby, Watford and Leyton Orient. However, our form before Len's arrival had been so dismal that we remained stuck in the relegation places. It looked as if we would need a miracle to stay up but a win away to Grimsby, in the penultimate game of the season, meant we still had a chance. Once again it went right down to the wire. If we could beat Luton Town at home, on the last day of the season, we would be safe.

Over ten thousand fans, the highest crowd of the season, turned up to see if we could perform yet another Houdini act. Luton were, however, a good team and although we were playing well, and had a vociferous crowd behind us, it was always going to be tough. We certainly didn't help matters in the early stages by playing really poorly, so poorly in fact that Luton raced to a 3–0 lead. For many supporters it was too much to take. Half of them left while the ones who stayed weren't shy in expressing their disgust. I was distraught and although we dug deep, and got two goals back from Kitch and Tarki, it wasn't enough. We were down.

In the circumstances I thought we had done really well to still be in with a shout of staying up but the club had pressed any number of self-destruct buttons. The season had been a disaster. In my opinion the effort needed to set up the rugby-league side had seen one or two take their eye off the ball as some of the decisions that the club made were nothing short of ludicrous.

We still had the chance to salvage something from the season by beating Swansea in the Welsh Cup final. Our Welsh Cup campaign that year had been an eventful one and we had to be at our best to beat our rivals Newport County and Wrexham. I will always remember the Wrexham game for the terrible abuse poor old Gary Stevens got from our supporters. Gary was a willing worker, and while he wasn't the most elegant player, he put in a shift and had a decent goal-scoring record. No matter which club you go to, however, the supporters always have a scapegoat and after a dreadfully disappointing campaign Gary had drawn the short straw. As the fans continued to chip away at his confidence his game slowly fell apart, which only served to make matters worse. Then, just as the abuse was at its peak, he managed to score. It was obvious that the stick had really got to him because when he celebrated he proceeded to stick two fingers up at the crowd.

I would never condone Gary's actions, but at the same time I could understand them. It must have been horrible for him to have thousands of people showering him with insults, especially his own fans. Some of the abuse was of a highly personal nature and I know that if I had heard that kind of thing I would have struggled to control myself. There was, however, no need to stick two fingers up at the crowd; he had already answered his critics by scoring. Gary's goal was followed up by a Peter Kitchen hat-trick and that earned us a semi-final tie against Hereford United. Although we beat Hereford over two legs, with Gary Stevens scoring the winner, the game at Edgar Street has always stayed in my mind, due to the trouble I saw in the stands. I stood and watched as an almighty punch-up broke out. Plenty more fans waded in and stewards and police struggled to keep it under control. Unfortunately, there were plenty of times in my career when I would be playing and out of the corner of my eye I could see it all kicking off. Sometimes I would even see fans fighting on my way into the ground when I was on the coach. It certainly made for an intimidating atmosphere.

During the 1970s and 1980s Cardiff may not have had an abundance of fans, but we did have a hardcore following, known of course as the Soul Crew, and they became just as well known for hooliganism as for being passionate supporters. Cardiff weren't the only club in the country with a hooligan firm – it seemed to be the fashion back then for every club to have one – but we undoubtedly had the most infamous gang.

Being a hooligan isn't something to be proud of but not all of those boys were thugs, or as evil as some liked to depict them. I knew a bloke from Canton, who everyone called Mad Frankie. He was a huge, ginger hulk – and by all accounts very handy in a scrap – but he was always good company and a devoted family man who would chop off his arm for you. I haven't got a clue why some of the supporters decided to get involved in hooliganism, but with the way the country was going in the early Eighties maybe they used football to let off steam. If I hadn't made it as a professional footballer I would have continued to watch Cardiff and, who knows, maybe I would have ended up getting caught up in it – or maybe not as I never liked getting hit! Don't get me wrong, I am glad that side of the game has now gone for good, and families can go to the football in peace, but the rivalry between the fans could be awesome at times and would get the grounds rocking.

Following the dramas against Wrexham and Hereford we were almost certainly guaranteed more fun and games in the final against Swansea. By this point we had already been relegated, but we were all determined to put one over on our neighbours, who had just enjoyed a fantastic season in the first division. The game at Ninian Park was an uneventful goalless draw and no one really fancied our chances at the Vetch. However, after Gary Bennett struck first, and Swansea went down to ten men, we suddenly felt that we had a great opportunity. However, it wasn't to be. Swansea were a fantastic side – with the likes of Leighton James, Alan Curtis and Bob Latchford in their ranks – and even with ten men they were too good for us, running out 2–1 winners.

It certainly hadn't been the best of seasons and there was no doubt that there needed to be wholesale changes. Sadly, I would be one of them.

# 17

# Down and Out?

Towards the back end of the previous season I started to have a few problems with my right knee. Earlier in my career I had of course had cartilage taken out and as a result I was now starting to suffer from arthritis. Training most days, and playing twice a week, would leave me in agony and sometimes I struggled to even bend my leg. With my knee continuing to deteriorate the club sent me to see a specialist, in Harley Street, to see if anything could be done to relieve the pain. The doctor's prognosis was bleak. Nothing could be done and if I continued to play I ran a real risk of ending up in a wheelchair. Given the circumstances he recommended that I retire.

I had realised that my knee wasn't in great shape, but the thought of packing in the game I loved scared me. Football was all that I knew. I had come in straight from school, with no qualifications, and had never had another job. As I was only thirty, I still thought that I had plenty of time before I had to contemplate a new career, but now that didn't appear to be the case. When I returned home I told Ann that I might have to retire and broke down. I was inconsolable. There was nothing else I wanted to do and I also had a wife and two kids I needed to support. I spent the night drenched in a cold sweat, dreading the future.

My knee wasn't 100 per cent, but despite the medical advice I felt that if I could tailor my training regime I might be able to continue. Ann didn't see it that way and she begged me to retire as she couldn't stand to see me cripple myself. Deep down I didn't think it would come to that. I thought the pain was manageable, and, if it became too much, then I would quit. It wasn't a decision I took lightly. After all, I didn't want my two children to grow up with their father confined to a wheelchair. Nevertheless I honestly felt I could play on without that happening. Foolish? Perhaps, but that's the path I took.

Following our relegation I went under the knife again to have more cartilage removed from my knee. I had the op as soon as the season was finished, and I hoped that I would have enough time to recuperate before pre-season started. One day, as I lay recuperating in my hospital bed, Ann came to visit and brought the *Echo* for me to read. Turning to the back page I saw that the headline predicted a summer clear out at the club. I had thought that Len would let a few go but I was interested to see who had got the chop. I knew I would be okay because the club hadn't been in contact with me, and I therefore assumed that my services would be required for the following season. However, when I scanned the article I was taken aback when I saw that my name was one on a long list of potential departures that included Peter Kitchen, Steve Grapes, Wayne Hughes, Tom Gilbert, Mick Henderson, Andy Polycarpou and Gary Stevens. The club were releasing me and they hadn't even let me know.

Although I was struggling to cope with my knee I thought that once I had the operation the club would give me a chance to prove my fitness. It was incomprehensible that after all these years of playing for City they would announce they were letting me go without so much as a by your leave. Sitting in that hospital bed, with my knee wrapped in bandages, and finding out that the club I loved had released me, was very difficult to accept. I hoped that another club would want me, but the odds were stacked against me. I was thirty years old with a bum knee and had just featured for a team that had been relegated. I was hardly a hot prospect.

After a few hours of feeling sorry for myself I decided that I wasn't going to take it lying down. First of all I was going to speak to Len to find out if the story was true, and, if it was, I would then do everything in my power to find another club. I was far from finished and knew I could do a job for someone if given the chance. On my release from hospital I went straight down to Ninian Park and made for Len's office. Both of us laid our cards on the table. I told him that

I felt I still had a part to play while he said that my knee had hindered my performances and that after reviewing my medical report, it was in my best interests to retire. It was disappointing, and although I believed that Len was wrong, we didn't fall out. We shook hands, and he wished me all the best. My time at Cardiff City was over.

Leaving the club I loved obviously upset me, but I didn't have time to dwell on it. With a family to support I had to get fit as quickly as possible if I was going to find a new employer. I had no time to lose so I turned my garage into a mini gym and every day I worked for hours strengthening my quads, which would in turn help to support my knee. Most of the time I put sandbags on my back and I did hundreds of squats, pushing myself to the point of exhaustion and beyond. The fact that some people thought I was finished spurred me on and I probably over-trained, such was my desperation to show the doubters that I wasn't ready for the scrapheap.

Beginning to fear the worst I got a phone call out of the blue from former City manager, Frank O'Farrell, who was now at Torquay with Bruce Rioch. Frank asked if I fancied meeting with Bruce and him to discuss a move. I jumped at the chance. It was not only nice to feel wanted but it was also great that after all these years Frank remembered me and thought I could do a job. The only problem was that I would only consider relocating to Torquay if Ann and the kids also fancied the move. Thankfully, they were excited at the prospect of living in one of Britain's most attractive seaside resorts and in my mind that was that. I was off.

From having no clubs interested in me I suddenly had two. Brian Godfrey, the Exeter City manager, had also heard that I had been released, and that I was due to travel to Torquay for talks. He asked if I would pop into Exeter on my way so that he could also have a chat about my future. Despite the fact I had virtually made up my mind I thought that I should at least listen to what Brian had to say before committing elsewhere. Ann and I subsequently met up with Brian in a hotel, and although he made me a very tempting offer, my gut feeling was that I wanted to give Torquay a shot.

Having met with Frank and Bruce I knew that I had made the right decision. I immediately felt at home. We agreed that it would be best if I played a few pre-season games before signing so that I could assess the club and they could have a closer look at me. I thought I did very well in the few games that I took part in. I was playing for my future and while some chose to stroll through the friendlies I treated each game as if it was my last. Unbeknown to me at the time, Cardiff had heard that I was looking back to my best, and had sent a scout to watch me play.

The scout obviously thought that I had done well because one day Len Ashurst called and asked if I would consider re-signing for Cardiff. It was truly astonishing. Just a few weeks previously he had strongly advised me to retire, believing I was finished. Now here he was, ready to offer me a new contract. Of course I went straight back to Cardiff and signed that same day.

Playing for Torquay had been great, and I have no doubt that if I had signed I would have enjoyed my time there, but Cardiff were my club and always would be. I certainly didn't want to end my time as a Bluebird on the back of a relegation. Frank and Bruce understood my decision, and wished me luck. I have to say that without their faith I may have packed in the game but they helped me prove to myself, and to others, that there was life in the old dog yet.

Astonishingly, I had made so much progress during the summer that Len even named me in his starting line-up for our first game of the season against Wrexham. The line-up was a much-changed one from the previous campaign, because after Len gave free transfers to a host of first-teamers, he brought in the likes of Jeff Hemmerman, David Tong, Roger Gibbins and Paul Bodin. Jeff was the sort of player we had been crying out for over the years. He was a hardworking forward, who could link up the play, as well as score all types of goals. I couldn't believe that his old club, Portsmouth, had let him go and I knew he would thrive on the quality balls Dave Bennett would provide from the right wing.

Whilst David Tong was a very good player he was so overweight we called him Mr Pillsbury. He was a squat little fella, with a big gut on him, and at first sight I couldn't believe that he was a professional footballer. To be honest Tongy worked his bollocks off that summer and within a few months he was at a decent playing weight. I remember that under his training gear he used to wear a black bin bag as a vest to help him sweat more. Tongy wasn't the silkiest of players, but every team needs people with a mixture of qualities and his contribution was to work hard, win the ball and then give it to Benno.

Len bought Roger Gibbins from Cambridge and he was another superb signing. Gibbo was a class act, a lovely midfield player with great touch and vision. He was definitely the beauty to Tongy's beast in our midfield. His passing ability was tremendous and he set up loads of Jeff's goals that season with passes that were threaded through the eye of a needle. Not only was he an asset on the pitch but he was also a great bloke off it, very friendly, always having a laugh, and would bet on just about anything. Over the years he has been a great servant to the club and he continues to work down there to this day.

Paul Bodin, on a free transfer from Newport, was another great addition. Len obviously knew all about Paul's qualities from his time at Newport, and while he was still a rough diamond, it was obvious that with a bit of work he could become a top player. Slotting in perfectly on our left-hand side he had one of the best left pegs I have ever seen, and he could ping the ball all over the pitch with uncanny accuracy. It was certainly no surprise to me that he went on to play in the Premier League and was part of that great Wales team of 1993 that came so close to reaching the World Cup finals, only for Paul to miss a vital penalty in the deciding qualifying game against Romania.

With so many new players in our line up to face Wrexham it took us a while to gel and as a result we ended up losing the game 2–1. I thought I had put in a decent shift, and certainly wasn't at fault for any of the goals, but Len obviously thought otherwise because he dropped me for the next game, away to Millwall. While I was gutted, I couldn't complain. The lads played out of their skins to win 4–0 at the Den.

Just as I thought I would struggle to get back into the team we then lost 4–0 away to Orient. Young Keith Pontin had a bit of a nightmare at the back, and although we then beat Wigan, 3–2, in the next game, he was again at fault for one of the goals. As a result Len decided to drop Keith for our game against Walsall and I was reinstated. I was obviously happy to be back but I felt sorry for Keith, as he was only a kid and his confidence had been knocked. Keith was a top prospect, who had played for Wales, and at one time had

Norwich, a first-division club, desperate to sign him. Surprisingly, that was, however, the end of him in professional football because after being dropped he decided to pack it in.

I always thought that he would come back at some point, but he never did. It was a real shame as Keith had the talent to enjoy a long career in the professional game, but to me he didn't want it enough. As we found with Robin Friday, while you have to be talented to make it in football a large part of being successful is down to how strong you are mentally. You have to be hungry to succeed and able to cope with the ups and downs that are part and parcel of a professional's life. I think Keith felt it wasn't a world he was going to enjoy so he walked away.

While the Walsall game marked the end of Keith's career it definitely was the rebirth of mine. We not only won 2–1 but I also managed to score the winner. It was a fairytale and although some of my friends and family said to me, 'You've shown them now Phil,' I didn't feel like that. I was just happy to be back playing for Cardiff City and scoring goals. I didn't feel any resentment towards anyone who thought my career was over. It was simply a huge relief to still be playing for the club I loved.

Following our win against Walsall we went on a great run, beating the likes of Sheffield United and Exeter City. It was becoming clear that Len had built a team that had all the ingredients needed for success. We had pace, skill, goal-scorers, creators, grafters and a wonderful team spirit. The team certainly had all the assets required to be promotion contenders and I was certain that once we had a chance to settle all of the new boys down we would take the division by storm.

On a high, following our run of good form, we added to the squad by signing Godfrey Ingram from San Jose Earthquakes for £200,000. Initially, this looked to be an astute bit of business. Godfrey was lightning quick with plenty of skill, and the supporters took to him immediately after he proceeded to score the winner on his debut against Gillingham. He certainly looked the real deal that day, but he faded badly, scoring only one more goal before being shipped back to San Jose, a few weeks later, for the same £200,000 fee. It was bizarre to say the least. Over the years the club had participated in what I thought were a few crazy transfers with clubs based in America. As I said earlier while I have no evidence whatsoever of any dodgy dealing I had my suspicions.

After we had beaten Bradford, 1–0, courtesy of a Gary Bennett goal, we shot to the top of the league. The players and the supporters had put up with years of relegation struggles so everyone was now enjoying Cardiff having a bit of success, even if it was only in the old third division. Everything was clicking at this point and in Jeff Hemmerman and Dave Bennett we had the top two players in the division. It has to be said that Len's record in the transfer market this season was outstanding. He hardly spent a penny but virtually every player he brought in was top notch.

Len made another astute signing after Godfrey Ingram left, when he brought in Bob Hatton on a free transfer from Sheffield United. Bob may have been getting on a bit but he gave us some invaluable experience and proved that he still knew where the back of the net was. Shortly after signing he even scored in four consecutive games, and our attacking axis of Bennett, Hemmerman and Hatton scared the life out of the opposition.

When we drew non-league Weymouth, at Ninian Park, in the second round of the FA Cup, I really fancied our chances of racking up a cricket score. We may have taken two ties to see off Wokingham Town in the first round but we were well into our stride by now and I couldn't see how part-timers could cope with us. After Gibbo and Jeff had put us into a two-goal lead we all thought that it was too easy so we took our foot off the gas. Football, however, has a habit of biting you on the ass if you don't put in 100 per cent and this game proved the point.

Coasting 2–0 at home, to a non-league team, we threw away the game and lost 3–2. It was criminal. I have to hold my hands up and admit that I was at fault for their winning goal, as I was caught in possession on the edge of the box. Ninian Park was not a nice place to be that day. It wasn't enough that the supporters tore strips off us at the final whistle, but they even waited for us at the main entrance after the game so they could continue their onslaught. Their abuse was nothing, however, compared to what Len Ashurst had to say. His pride obviously wounded, he went ballistic. We had to sit there and take it. We had no excuses.

Thankfully, while we disgraced ourselves in the Cup, our league form was good over December. We were still top of the table come Christmas when we faced a derby game, against Newport, who were also challenging for promotion. Jeff and Bob put us 2–0 up, and we were cruising, but late on Newport somehow pulled two goals back and it looked as though we would have to settle for a point. Just as the crowd started to head for the exits Jeff was put through on goal and dramatically lobbed the keeper to win the game. There were over fifteen thousand fans in the ground and it had been a long time since I had heard a goal celebrated so loudly. Everyone was aware that it was not only an important goal, in terms of putting one over on our rivals, but it also put us in a great position in the league.

By now, with the team earning a deserved reputation for playing attractive, winning football, the fans came back in their droves. Over the past few years we had struggled to get crowds in excess of ten thousand, despite playing at a higher level. Now we were regularly getting crowds of that amount, and more. It was brilliant to have the feel-good factor around the place again.

Despite still getting pain in my knee I didn't think that it was affecting my performances. Len allowed me to miss training if I needed to rest and I was also getting through a regular cocktail of pills and injections to get myself ready for games. It wasn't ideal but once a game kicked off the adrenalin took over and I barely noticed it. Sometimes the knee would swell up, and it gave me many sleepless nights, but that was a small price to pay to still be turning out for Cardiff City.

After Christmas we kept up our promotion push with wins over Brentford, Walsall, Exeter and Millwall, as well as crushing our promotion rivals, Oxford United, 3–0. We couldn't keep that sort of form up all the time though and in February we lost 4–2 to Bradford. It was a strange game, because, due to injury, our goalkeeper, Andy Dibble, had to go off. I deputised in goal for a bit, keeping a clean sheet, before Linden Jones took over the custodian's role. Once I was back outfield I was then pushed up front, as we were chasing the game, and I proceeded to score! Amazingly, I had now played in just about every position for Cardiff.

Confidence was high, and at times we felt unbeatable, but the final few months of the season stretched our small squad to the limit as injuries, fatigue and loss of form hit us. In the space of ten games we only won twice, and drew home matches against Reading and Bournemouth, as well as at promotion rivals, Portsmouth. Slowly but surely we were being caught at the top of the table, and, on 4 April we faced a real test: Newport County at Somerton Park. If we lost then they would go top.

John Aldridge was still at Newport, and although we had kissed and made up, we still enjoyed kicking each other all over the pitch. This time around I didn't kick him hard enough because he managed to score the only goal of the game. We had spent most of the season at the top, but now, with just a few weeks remaining, we had been caught and even faced the prospect of missing out on promotion altogether.

That loss hit us all hard. We had to have a long look in the mirror and ask how much we wanted it. Yes, we were suffering from injuries and fatigue, but great teams roll up their sleeves at times like that and fight for the win. This squad was, however, made of stern stuff and while we didn't play the free-flowing football we were capable of in those final few games, we did grind out results. In fact we went the last seven games of the season unbeaten and our last home game, against Leyton Orient, gave us the chance to seal promotion.

Early on things went in our favour when Orient were reduced to ten men. John Lewis and Benno took full advantage as they both scored to put us in the driving seat. Orient showed little ambition. I think they just wanted to keep the score down. We were quite happy with our lead and so we saw out the game with some neat possession football. At the final whistle thousands of fans flooded onto the field and lifted the players shoulder high.

During my career I was lucky to have been involved with a few Ninian Park pitch invasions to celebrate promotion, or narrowly escaping relegation, but this one was extra special. Precisely a year earlier I had been told that my career was over and that never again would I play for my beloved team. Never in my wildest dreams did I think that I would play an integral part in a promotion-winning Cardiff City team. I stayed out on the pitch with the supporters for as long as possible. I was determined to soak it up and to remember all of their smiling faces and their messages of goodwill. Who knows, maybe Len would think that I couldn't cut it in the second division, and would release me again. I had learnt to savour every moment of my time as a Bluebird because you never knew if the next game would be your last.

There was a lovely atmosphere in the players' lounge after the game. The wives and kids joined us for a big celebration and after a few drinks I got quite emotional, telling people I loved them and all of that. Credit where it is due, Len Ashurst had worked miracles and that promotion was very much down to him.

Although we had achieved promotion we still had one game remaining, away to Bristol Rovers. Neither team had anything to play for so it looked as if we would enjoy a stroll in the sun and that would be that. If only that had been the case. Over the course of the season Jeff Hemmerman had been a vital part of our success, scoring twenty-two goals and working brilliantly alongside Bob Hatton. He had nothing to prove against Bristol, but he was a wholehearted player who would never pull out of a challenge, even in a meaningless game. Faced with a fifty-fifty challenge with their goalkeeper he didn't hold back. As soon as I heard him scream, and saw his crumpled right leg, I knew he was in trouble. Poor Jeff had torn the cruciate ligament in his knee. These days most players can get back playing within six to eight months of such an injury, but back then it was a potential career ender. It was sickening to think that after such a tremendous season Jeff might never make it back onto a football pitch.

The season may have ended on a sour note for Jeff, but for Cardiff City, and me, it had been one to remember. I was already looking forward to the start of the next season, as long as Len still wanted me around.

# 18

# Rollercoaster

It turned out that I had no need to worry about getting a new contract at Cardiff. Len offered me a new one-year deal, which I was grateful for. It was great that he had not only rewarded me for my performances but also thought that I could still do a job at a higher level. Having performed miracles on a shoestring budget, I was hoping that the club would give Len some decent money to spend. In previous years, in the second division, we had never been able to have a proper go as we were always selling our best players. Surely, I thought, the board would see we now had a manager, and a squad, that were going places and would give us every chance of success by freeing up some money. I was to be proved wrong.

With the Cardiff Blue Dragons rugby-league side continuing to be a millstone round the club's neck all available funds were diverted to help prop them up. At this stage the rugby team were averaging crowds of about six hundred, and it was obvious that the experiment hadn't worked, but rather than shut them down the club tried in vain to administer the kiss of life on an already dead patient.

While we weren't able to spend much money I thought that if we managed to keep our squad together than we were at least a mid-table team at this level. Unfortunately, it was not to be. Jeff Hemmerman had of course picked up a serious injury, and we would be lucky to see him again that season, if ever. Bob Hatton then decided to retire, which left us with only Dave Bennett for the striking positions.

Benno had been fantastic for us, and had plenty of clubs clamouring for his services, but I thought that with Bob and Jeff out of the picture we had to keep hold of him if we wanted to avoid a season of struggle. Frustratingly, first division Coventry City then entered the picture, and made a bid of £120,000 for his services. An offer of that size proved to be too tempting for our cash-strapped club to resist, and without further ado Benno was off. All of a sudden we had no forwards.

Len hoped that at the very least he would be able to spend some of the money we had received but was told that he would again have to make do with free transfers. His efforts the previous year had been miraculous but for him to do it again, at a higher level, was a big ask. Getting on with the job he scoured the country for bargains and eventually signed Gordon Owen from Sheffield Wednesday, Gary Plumley from Newport County and Chris Rodin from Brighton, on loan. All of them were very nice guys, but not a patch on Bob, Benno and Jeff.

Just as I thought the state of the club couldn't get any worse we were told that chairman, Bob Grogan, had terminal cancer and had to step down. While I hadn't agreed with all Bob's decisions I loved him to bits as a bloke and appreciated that without his investment Cardiff City could have gone under. I don't think the supporters ever realised just how much of his own money, and effort, Bob had put into the club. His decisions weren't always popular, but we respected him immensely. He was just a nice guy who loved football. Shortly after stepping down Bob passed away and his business partner, Jack Leonard took over. We were lucky that there was a ready-made replacement already at the club and I was sure that we would be in good hands with Jack at the helm.

Going into the new season we were in disarray on and off the pitch. From bitter experience I knew that if you were going to do well at this level you had to be well prepared. Losing 2–0 to Charlton on the opening day wasn't much of a surprise, neither was the fact that we failed to score. In fact our inability to score goals was a huge problem as we didn't trouble the scoreboard in nine out of our first thirteen games. From being renowned for our high-scoring, free-flowing football we were now trying our best to keep the score down and nick a goal whenever we could. Predictably, this was not the type of football supporters enjoy and, for some games, our crowds dropped to around five thousand.

On 29 September 1983 Len decided to go for broke and entered into an amazing player swap with Newport County that would see five players changing clubs. Leaving Cardiff were Linden Jones, Tarki Micallef and John Lewis while joining us were Nigel Vaughan and Karl Elsey. It was a move that surprised me. Nigel and Karl were good players, but they weren't much better than the boys we lost and, more importantly, neither were prolific goal scorers. We were in dire need of someone to put the ball in the back of the net and in all honesty I thought this was a missed opportunity to sign someone who could do just that.

While Len eventually brought in a striker, Phil Walker, on loan from Rotherham, it didn't work out as he failed to score a single goal during his spell with us. Gordon Owen started to settle, and was popping up with the odd goal, but he wasn't an out-and-out goal scorer as he preferred to play a lot deeper. What really frustrated me was that it wasn't as if we were leaking lots of goals. If Jeff hadn't got injured, and we had kept Benno, then I was sure that we would have been looking up the table rather than scrapping for our lives.

Out of nowhere we managed a freak result against Cambridge United on 12 November, hammering them 5–0, with Gordon Owen and Gibbo scoring two each and Nigel Vaughan grabbing the other. It was not, however, a sign that we were about to enjoy a good period of form as we then proceeded to win just once in five games before we faced Swansea. Our age-old rivals had lasted just two seasons in the first division and much to the delight of our fans had been relegated the previous year. We met them at Ninian Park, on Boxing Day, and although neither side was in great form we certainly gave our supporters a Christmas treat with our best display of the season. Just days before the game we had signed Trevor Lee, a big, bustling forward from Bournemouth. Big Trev became an instant hit with the fans as he scored the winner against the Jacks. We all hoped that he could continue scoring goals, but although he got a few more over the course of the season, he didn't turn out to be the answer to our prayers.

Early in 1984 Jeff Hemmerman stepped up his rehab and tried to make a return to action. I could tell in training that he still didn't look right but Jeff was understandably keen to get back as soon as possible and Len welcomed the prospect of his return. After a few games, in which Jeff had really struggled, it was clear that he was never going to be the player he once was. The injury had robbed him of a yard of pace and he also couldn't turn sharply. It was a crying shame, but it was no surprise when he decided to retire. Everyone had been hoping that once Jeff had returned to fitness we would start scoring goals, but with his career over the search for a quality attacker continued.

Desperate to find a goal scorer Len gave a lad called Martin Goldsmith a trial. Such was our dearth of forwards he even named him on the bench for our game against Middlesbrough. With the game tied at 1–1, Len threw Martin on and he proceeded to score the winner. The lads were delighted with the win and by Martin's goal, but they also got a right good laugh at his expense. The fact was that he bore an uncanny resemblance to Worzel Gummidge, which of course we had to point out to him. He didn't take offence and laughed it off as we celebrated with him after the game.

Amazingly, the day after our win over Middlesbrough the club was rocked by the news that Len Ashurst had resigned to take over at Sunderland. While I couldn't believe that Len had gone in the middle of a relegation fight I couldn't blame him for going to Sunderland. He had enjoyed a successful playing career for the club and it was clear that he still had a lot of affection for them. There was no doubt they were a team on the up, one with money to spend, and were at that time a considerably more attractive proposition than Cardiff.

There were just two months of the season remaining, and, with the team fighting for their lives, it was vital that the club brought in the right man. For a brief period I considered applying for the job myself. I reasoned that no one cared about Cardiff more than me and that I knew the squad well and could do the job. However, I was still enjoying playing too much and thought that the club would probably want to appoint an experienced manager at a time like this so I didn't go for it.

When I heard that the club had appointed trainer, Jimmy Goodfellow, and midfielder, Jimmy Mullen, on a temporary basis, I suppose I was a little disappointed that I hadn't been asked. After all, I had been at the club for a lot longer and felt that I had just as much management potential as either of them. While I was a little put out I vowed to give the two Jimmys everything I had. This wasn't a time to have a sulk, but to roll up my sleeves and reassess in the summer.

One of their first games in charge was an incredible match against Chelsea. We played some brilliant football for the first eighty minutes and goals from Gibbo, Owen and Vaughan put us into a three-goal lead. Chelsea's fans, unhappy at the roasting we were giving their team, started to kick off and tried to cause trouble. With the stadium on the brink of a riot they soon had reason to concentrate on the game, as we inexplicably collapsed, allowing them to score three goals in the final ten minutes.

Losing a winning lead seemed to be a habit, because we then went on to blow a two-goal lead at the Vetch and lost 3–2. That was a sickener and questions were asked about our bottle, fitness and awareness. I can't put my finger on it to be honest, even now. If anything I think it came down to a lack of confidence. Facing an onslaught we started to panic, and once we conceded the one goal, everyone stopped doing the basics and started making crazy decisions.

Usually, I was a real hate figure at the Vetch, as I was a Cardiff boy who never hid his love for his club. I couldn't repeat some of the things I have been called by Swansea supporters on a football pitch, but it is all part of the game. You just brush it off and get on with it. During this game I remember that the fans were really letting me have it so I tried to defuse the situation. At the time Swansea's kit was made by a manufacturer called Patrick. I always wore Patrick boots so when I was near the North Bank stand I pointed to the Patrick symbol on my boots and gave the thumbs up. That made them laugh and for a brief moment they even stopped chanting 'Dwyer, you're a wanker'.

We may have been throwing away vital points, but thankfully the teams below us were doing even worse. In the last five games we won just once but remarkably we finished in fifteenth place. I knew that this was, however, just papering over the cracks. If we continued in the same vein of form the following season there was no doubt that we would go down.

# 19

# Record Breaker

The 1984/85 campaign was to be my fourteenth as a professional at Cardiff City. I now thought every new season could be my last so I was always grateful for a new contract and determined to show that I could still cut it. My knee had continued to deteriorate but I still felt that it wasn't yet at the point where I would have to consider retirement. If I continued to work hard on building up my quads, and rested when necessary, I thought I could enjoy another two to three years in the game.

If the club was going to avoid another stressful season they needed to sort out the managerial situation as quickly as possible. Jimmy Goodfellow was eventually offered a permanent contract and, although he had kept us up, I was surprised the club looked to him. Our survival hadn't been due to our own good form but because some teams played even worse.

One thing, however, that I had learned during my fourteen years was that it was very difficult to judge which managers would do well and which would fail. For instance, everyone was convinced that Frank O'Farrell would be brilliant but his time at the club wasn't the best while no one gave Richie Morgan a chance and yet he led us to ninth place in the second division. I hoped that Jimmy would exceed expectations and despite my reservations he had my full support.

If Jimmy was to make an impact the club would have to give him money to buy new players. We still didn't have an out-and-out goal scorer in the squad and we also needed reinforcements in other areas.

In previous seasons the rugby-league side had stopped us spending, but this year the board finally saw sense and pulled the plug. It was obvious the venture had failed and that the club could no longer afford to prop it up. Not only was that beneficial for the football club's finances, but it was also good news for the Ninian Park pitch.

These days the Cardiff Blues rugby-union team shares the new stadium with Cardiff City. Although playing both sports there does affect the pitch there is technology in place, and a team of grounds-men, to ensure that it never gets too bad. In my day there were no weaved pitches or high-tech lighting to help the pitch recover – all we had were pitchforks! As a result the pitch was a nightmare and it became impossible to play football as the ball bobbled all over the place. With the rugby team gone I knew that I would no longer have to fear looking like a mug with an attempted pass bobbling off my boot and being sliced into the crowd.

I am sure Jimmy felt that with the rugby club gone he would be able to spend some money, and keep the squad together, but it didn't turn out that way. Firstly, the club sold Andy Dibble to Luton for £125,000; then Gary Bennett joined up with Len Ashurst at Sunderland for £75,000 before Gordon Owen departed to Barnsley for £27,000. All three had been among our better performers the previous season and replacing them was going to be hard work, especially if none of the money was going to reach Jimmy. As had been the case in previous years, the board kept the transfer money and Jimmy had to make do with free transfers. He did his best by bringing in Vaughan Jones from Newport, Kevin Summerfield from Walsall, John Seasman from Rotherham and Lee Smelt from Halifax Town. But despite the new recruits it was always going to be a thank-less task.

It was hoped that Kevin would solve our problems up front, John would be a good source of supply from the wing, while Vaughan at the back, and Lee in goal, would help make us difficult to beat. On paper it sounded great, but would they improve us? My question was answered emphatically on the opening day of the season when we were atrocious and were well beaten, 3–0, by Charlton Athletic, at Ninian Park. Again the same old problems resurfaced, leaking goals at the back, hesitant in midfield and misfiring in front of goal.

Jimmy must have realised that we were nowhere near good enough because that result prompted him to look for more new players. He brought in Paul Bannan on loan from Bristol, who didn't last long, as it was clear it wasn't going to make a difference, and he also promoted goalkeeper Mel Rees from the youth team. Mel was only a young lad – from Grangetown, like me – and I always had a lot of time for him. I felt that given a few years of experience he had all the attributes needed to be a very good keeper but it was a tough ask to come in and do a job that season, even though he would get plenty of practice shot stopping! Tragically, we never got to see Mel fulfil his potential because he died from cancer in his twenties. In the games he did play, I think he showed that he definitely had what it took to reach the top and it is such a shame he is no longer with us.

One signing that caused a stir was that of former England captain, Gerry Francis. In his prime Gerry had been one of the top players in the country and, despite being well into his thirties, I felt that his quality on the ball could still make a huge difference. In his short spell with us Gerry was a great guy to have around. As I expected he was a true professional, who really set an example. He could have taken it easy but he slogged his guts out in training and put everything he had into games. His best days were long gone but what he had left was still more than good enough for us.

Unfortunately, Gerry only played a handful of games before moving on. I think he was not only struggling to settle in the area but could also see that the club was in a real state. I remember that one day we were training at the old Civil Service ground and Gerry and I were having a chat about how things were going at the club. We both agreed that unless money was spent we would do well to avoid relegation. The writing was on the wall as far as I was concerned and people needed to stop putting their heads in the sand and realise that something drastic needed to be done.

I felt for Jimmy, who was no doubt panicking a bit. He knew he couldn't spend any money so had no option but to bring in guys on frees, and on trial, in the hope that one of them could offer us something. At least he was giving it a go, in very tough circumstances, but it seemed it was a case of quantity rather than quality.

When recently relegated Leeds United came to Ninian Park on 12 September we were rock bottom and no one gave us a chance against the supposed best team in the division. Throughout my career I always played to win, and never approached a game feeling we had no chance, but I knew that it would be an uphill battle to get anything from Leeds. My hero, and nemesis, Billy Bremner, had long since retired, which was a shame as I still felt that I owed him one after he talked down to me when we had played them in the FA Cup all those years ago. On the day we played our best football for months and at times Leeds couldn't cope. Winning the game 2–1, I was thrilled to score the deciding goal against my boyhood idols. Just when you think you've done everything you wanted to in the game football continues to surprise you.

Could this performance have been the catalyst to drag us out of trouble? No, it turned out to be a freak result because we then lost five on the bounce. One of those losses, at Blackburn, turned out to be a bittersweet experience for me. Conceding a last-minute goal was a real kick in the teeth, but it also marked the day that I broke Tom Farquharson's appearance record of 445 games for Cardiff City. I was obviously thrilled to have broken the record but it would have been so much sweeter if I could have marked the occasion with a win.

To be honest, while I knew that I had played a lot of games for Cardiff, I didn't have a clue that I was close to breaking the record. Neither did anyone at the club because no one mentioned anything to me. I don't think anyone realised until the supporters club marked the occasion by presenting me with a commemorative plaque. I was happy it was the supporters who made the presentation. Throughout my career I had enjoyed a very strong bond with the fans. I think that was partly due to the fact that if I hadn't made it as player I would have been standing on the terraces with them. After all, I was a local boy, a City fan, and I counted myself lucky to have played one game for Cardiff let alone hundreds. Playing for the club you love and support is an honour many would give their right arm for and I was mindful of that every time I pulled on the blue jersey.

One reason I think the fans took to me was that I used to love a bit of banter with them. I remember that during a game with Newport, at Somerton Park, the Cardiff end was so overcrowded that stewards took a young girl out of the crowd and walked her along the side of the pitch. Boys will be boys and some of them started to chant, 'Get your tits out for the lads.' Despite it being in the middle of the game I turned to the fans, and pulled my top up to reveal my chest. Not a pretty sight but it gave us all a laugh.

So how did I manage to stay at the club for so long and play so many games? I really don't know, because I wasn't the best player at the club, but I like to think that I always gave my all and that always stands you in good stead in any walk of life. Another important factor was that over the years I had worked very hard on my game and I think I made the most of my ability. Looking back I am so proud that I hold the appearance record, especially as Jimmy Scoular came so close to releasing me, as did Len Ashurst. I am glad that I never gave up on the club, or on football, when it might have been easier to walk away. When I started my career I would never have dreamt in a million years that I would go on to play more games than anyone else has ever done for the club. Even now when people raise the subject I still have to pinch myself. It seems inconceivable, but it is something I am very proud of.

Following my record-breaking game at Blackburn we were then soundly trounced, 3–0, at home to Manchester City. Jimmy was at his wits' end and snapped when speaking to the press after the game. He told the reporters, 'The board said money would be made available for the right players. I recommended certain players but all were rejected for one reason or another.' What Jimmy said was true but as soon as I heard him speak those words I knew he wouldn't last much longer. I had a lot of sympathy for him. He was fighting for his life in his first job in management and he wasn't getting a lot of help. He had inherited a poor squad, there was no money to spend and the board was selling his best players from under his feet. At the same time the club was broke, and had to cut its cloth accordingly, and he knew this when he took the job. It is always easy to say in hindsight, but, after Len had left, the club should have looked for someone with experience and contacts in the game, someone who could have picked up good players on loan and free transfers. With it being Jimmy's first job that was never going to be one of his strengths. Neither he nor the club were in a good place and I remember thinking that the writing was on the wall.

Unsurprisingly, Jimmy was sacked a few days after the Man City result and the club was yet again looking for a new manager. We certainly weren't an inviting prospect: rock bottom of the league and with no money to spend. The new man would have his work cut out. Again, I was briefly tempted to toss my hat into the ring but I still wanted to play and felt that with the club in the state it was in I would be fighting a losing battle as a rookie manager.

If the new manager was going to save us he needed three qualities above all others: he had to be able to bring in good players on the cheap; he had to be tactically astute; he needed to be an excellent motivator. The question was: with our limited resources how were we going to find such a paragon?

After a short wait the board eventually announced that it had appointed Alan Durban as the new manager. Alan was a former Cardiff player who had also managed Shrewsbury, Stoke and Sunderland. He had been in the game for a long time, he knew the club inside out and in addition he was well respected. Given our circumstances I thought it was the best appointment we could have hoped for. Another positive factor, from a purely personal point of view, was that I knew Alan rated me, because he had tried to sign me when he was in charge at Stoke.

In Alan's first week in charge he called me into his office and asked me how morale was. I didn't pull any punches and said that the spirit was as good as could be expected but the boys definitely could do with a lift. He decided that it would be a good idea if we all went out for a meal, and had a few drinks, to relieve the tension and get to know one another. I thought it was a cracking idea so I arranged for us to go to the Captain's Wife, down Sully, after training on the Friday. Everyone really enjoyed themselves and Alan, who was a hard man and one you didn't want to cross, came over very well. It was just what we needed.

We may have lost our first two games under Alan, against Middlesbrough and Portsmouth, but we all knew there would be no quick fix and that he needed time to settle. He immediately started to look for players and brought back Tarki Micallef from Newport, and signed Wales international Brian Flynn. During my time in the Wales squad I had played alongside Brian and I knew that he was capable.

Now, in the later stages of his career, he wasn't the player he once was but he was comfortable on the ball and very experienced. It is amazing how things turn out. Back then I would never have thought that Brian would be a success as a manager. For a start he never struck me as the management type, and he was also so small that I thought he would struggle to gain respect in a dressing room, but he has well and truly proved me wrong. Over the years Brian has done a cracking job as a manager at club and international level and I take my hat off to him.

Tarki and Brian were good players, who would do a job for us, but once again the problem of scoring goals remained. Kevin Seasman wasn't setting the world alight up top and the only person we could rely on for goals was midfielder Nigel Vaughan, who was playing very well. Players continued to roll into the club as Alan tried desperately to find a solution. In came David Felgate, Kevin Meacock, Mike Ford, Paul McLoughlin and Graham Withey. None of them were any better than what we had already but I suppose they were bodies who could add competition for places and keep people on their toes.

Despite an abundance of new faces our performances didn't improve and we won only once in Alan's first six games in charge. Crowds slumped to the three thousand mark, which certainly didn't help finances or morale. Who could blame the fans? We were not playing well and the south Wales economy was in real difficulty, particularly in the valleys where a lot of our support has always come from. No man is going to spend his limited money on going to the football when he has a family to support and the product on offer is abysmal.

Those that did turn up weren't very appreciative of our efforts and one game, against Oldham, saw them really go for the jugular as we went 2–0 down. As there were so few in the ground you could hear every insult and I don't mind admitting that it hurt, even if we were playing crap. Just as I thought we would need a police escort to get us off the pitch without being lynched, Nigel Vaughan scored twice to save us. It was desperately sad to see the club in such a sorry state, but for years we had survived on a shoestring, continually selling our best players and not replacing them. This was the year in which the watch-the-pennies policy fell flat on its face.

Vaughny's two goals against Oldham gave us a boost and in the next game Tongy struck an injury-time winner to see us beat Carlisle. It was nice to see that despite our lack of quality we were rolling up our sleeves and refusing to go without a fight. In my heart, however, I knew it wouldn't be enough. We fought hard but we couldn't escape the fact that we just didn't have what it took to compete effectively. After the win at Carlisle, on 17 November, we didn't win again until 2 February. We were well adrift of safety at that point and by the time we beat Middlesbrough, in front of our lowest post-war crowd of 2,562, we were virtually down and out. Ninian Park felt like a morgue that day. Losing 6–3 to Grimsby all but sealed our fate, but amazingly we then beat Charlton 4–1 at the Valley. I scored our fourth, but I wasn't to know it would be my last for the club.

On 17 February 1985 I played what turned out to be my last game for Cardiff City, against Notts County, at Ninian Park. It is a day I would rather forget. Going down 4–1 at home is always hard to bear, particularly when you have had a nightmare, and were culpable for a few of the goals. I had not played well, and I was bitterly disappointed, but at least I had given my all. In the circumstances it hadn't been enough, but at no point did I concede defeat. However, I believe that some on the pitch that day did jack it in. In my eyes that wasn't acceptable. I don't care if you're not the best player in the world, as long as you give everything you have, in every game that you play; no one can ask for more than that. On the day, for whatever reason – lack of confidence, tiredness, not getting on with the manager – some went into hiding.

It is fair to say that I wasn't in the best of moods as I walked off the pitch to another chorus of boos. I was incredibly frustrated at my own display and was seething at the performance of others. Walking into the dressing room I expected everyone to be as angry as myself, but while some were deathly quiet others were chatting away as if nothing untoward had happened. As the captain of the team I felt it was my duty to say something. While I didn't name names I let rip and made it crystal clear that we had let ourselves down out there, myself included. If there were some who didn't have the stomach for a relegation fight, or who felt that they couldn't put in 100 per cent any more, then they should hold their hands up and walk away.

Not everyone was guilty – some of the boys just had their confidence shot to pieces, and were making basic errors – but I felt it was time that we had a harsh reality check. Over the weekend I suggested that everyone take a long hard look at themselves and come in Monday morning ready to start afresh.

Alan wasn't best pleased with my speech and he took the view that it would do more harm than good. My response was that I failed to see how we could get any worse, and that something needed to be said. We needed a giant kick up the backside, I told him. He said to me, 'You can't talk anyway Phil. You didn't cover yourself in glory out there.' I agreed with his analysis of my performance and acknowledged that every single one of us had to hold our hands up and admit that on the day, from top to bottom, we had not been good enough. Alan and I didn't have a big row, just a frank exchange of views. It was obvious that we were both hurting and doing our best, in our own way, to get the club moving in the right direction. I wasn't questioning his authority, I just felt that there was a time and a place for a captain to have his say and this had been one of them.

When I turned up at Ninian Park on the Monday morning I certainly didn't think that there would be any repercussions about my little speech in the dressing room, but I was wrong. On arrival Alan called me into his office. I assumed we were going to clear the air, but what he told me felt like a punch to the gut. He said that the manager of Rochdale, Vic Hallom, had been on the phone and wanted to sign me. I asked if that was what he wanted and he replied that it was for the best as I no longer figured in his plans.

It was too much to take in.

I honestly thought I would finish my career at Cardiff and could never envisage playing anywhere else. The thought of leaving at this stage in my career had never entered my mind. I had hoped that once I retired that I could stay on at the club in some capacity, either as a coach, manager or even as the kit man. That was how much the club meant to me. I would have taken any job just to have prolonged my association with this great club, but now that would not be possible.

I was also disappointed that Alan had felt it necessary to get rid of me because of what I had said. It was true, I hadn't played well, but there had been plenty who were as bad as me that day and they weren't being released. Did he think I was undermining him or, per-haps, that I was a threat to his position? I don't know, but he was the boss and if he didn't want me around there wasn't much I could do.

Not once did the thought of retirement enter my mind. Maybe it should have done. I was in my thirties, my knee was in a bad way and my best days appeared to be behind me. But I loved the game so much I would have played with one leg. I firmly believed I still had a bit left in the tank and if someone was willing to sign me I would give it everything I had.

Once the shock of being told that I wasn't wanted by Cardiff had worn off I asked Alan for Vic Hallom's number so that I could have a chat with him. I had a lot of respect for Vic – he had been part of the Sunderland team that had won the FA Cup – and I had played against him a few times. He had been at Rochdale for a few years now, with Johnny King as his assistant, and although the team had struggled I thought I would enjoy playing for both men.

After discussing the move with Ann – who wasn't best pleased that I might have to move – I set off to Rochdale for talks. Dave Grant, a Cardiff teammate whom Rochdale also wanted to sign, joined me on the trip north. Vic was an infectious character who made you think that anything was possible and once we had talked I knew I would enjoy playing at Spotland. They may have been in the old fourth divi-sion, and at the wrong end of the table, but Vic really motivated me. I felt wanted, which was important, and without further ado I signed. Amazingly, I was on more money at Rochdale, a fourth-division side, than I had been at Cardiff, who were two leagues above them.

Perhaps I had been a bit rash signing so quickly, without properly evaluating my options, because I soon learned that both Swansea and Newport wanted to talk to me. Alan Durban, however, hadn't told me about their interest. No doubt he didn't want me to play for a club in south Wales, but I would have appreciated the opportunity to at least discuss it. Playing for Swansea had never entered my mind, but the thought intrigued me. I would have loved to have seen what reaction I would have got from their fans, and from Cardiff's, if I had ever returned to Ninian Park as a Jack. Plenty of players have crossed the great divide over the years so I think it would have worked out, but I'll never know.

Not being told of the approaches from Swansea and Newport was disappointing but what really angered me was when I was told afterwards that Alan wanted me out as he thought I was a bad influence. If he had thought I was rubbish, or past it, fair enough, but to hear that he thought I upset the dressing room really got under my skin. If you ask any player or manager that I had ever been associated with I am sure they would say that I had always set a good example. My tirade after the Notts County game obviously ruffled Alan's feathers but it wasn't done to undermine him and during my time at the club I had certainly heard a lot worse.

With my future now at Rochdale I turned my attention to fighting relegation with them but I still kept my eye on Cardiff's results. Predictably, they finished rock bottom of the table and were relegated well before the end of the season. It was the end of an era and I wondered just where both of us would end up.

# 20

# Rochdale

As I had only signed a contract with Rochdale until the end of the 1984/85 season I didn't have to move up north, which was a relief to my family. Cardiff allowed Dave Grant and me to train with the youth team during the week, and then on a Friday we would travel up to Rochdale, to train with our new teammates, before playing on the Saturday. It was a new experience for me, but I found that it worked well. Not having to uproot my family was obviously very important, particularly when I didn't know if I would be playing for Rochdale beyond the end of the season. Training at Cardiff was a bit strange at first, but because of the state of my knee I didn't have to go in every day and a lot of the time, when I did go in, I worked by myself. By now I knew exactly how to prepare myself for games and how to look after my knee.

On Fridays, when Dave and I arrived in Rochdale, Vic would usually name the team for our game the next day. Following that we would then work on how we were going to be set up and practise defensive and attacking set pieces. I was surprised at how organised Vic and his staff were. They certainly weren't mugs and I felt they had all the attributes of a good management team. The boys at Rochdale were great and it didn't take me long to get involved in the changing-room banter. No matter which club you go to you will find that by and large the jokes and gags are the same. You can guarantee that there will always be a nutter, a practical joker and a pretty boy and that jokes will be made about a player's height, weight, sexual preference and playing ability (or lack of it). By the end of my career I had tried-and-trusted banter for each one of these areas.

One of the guys who I struck up a rapport with, on and off the pitch, was an enormous centre half called Joe Cook. Joe was the biggest guy I had ever seen on a football pitch. He must have been six-four and he was built like a wrestler. Sometimes big players aren't as strong as they look but Big Joe was a beast, and he loved nothing more than getting stuck in. Bloody hell, we had some fun together. We used to frighten the life out of people. If an opposition player got past one of us the other would be waiting with a nice welcome present. We were football's version of the Krays, except that we didn't have knuckledusters, only the sharpened studs on our boots.

Another good guy I remember from my time at Rochdale was Shaun Reid, the brother of Everton legend Peter. Shaun was just like Peter, always in the middle of any mischief, and he just would not stop talking. When you were in the mood it was great, but even on a long coach journey home after a defeat he would still be at it. He loved being the centre of attention and he was a top bloke who by and large was great company.

After training Dave and I would set off to our accommodation for the night, which was a pub on the outskirts of Rochdale. It was far from glamorous. It seems unbelievable now that a football club would put its players up in a pub but we definitely didn't complain. In fact we couldn't believe our luck. It was only a little place, with just the three bedrooms upstairs, but it was cosy and it reminded me of the Woolpack in *Emmerdale*. The landlord was always happy to see Dave and me, and he would often join us for a drink before going to bed. He always used to say that we could stay downstairs for as long as we liked, and, if we wanted a drink, to help ourselves and leave the money on the counter. Sometimes Dave and I were tempted to really go for it, but as we always had a game the next day we usually just had the one pint before retiring.

These days alcohol is of course frowned upon in the professional game. In my day it was encouraged and if you didn't drink you were an outcast. Everyone enjoyed a drink; it was seen as a vital part of team bonding. Our diets and preparation were nothing compared to what they are today. Don't get me wrong, we were all fit lads, certainly compared to the majority of the population, but there is no way we could have played today with habits like that. The players of today are athletes and their meticulous approach to looking after their bodies has taken playing standards to new heights. I love football so much I don't think I would have had a problem refining my diet but I certainly know of one or two who would never have made it. (Tongy, I wasn't thinking of you, honest!)

When my wife found out I was staying in a pub she wasn't too happy. I think she thought I was having her on and that I was really staying in the Hilton so I told her to come up with me and have a look. To say that she wasn't impressed is an understatement. From the moment we got to Rochdale to the moment we left she didn't stop moaning.

In the first place she didn't like the cramped room we shared above the pub, then she didn't like the fact it rained all the time, but what really got her back up was when she came to see me play at Spotland. While she was reading her book in the players' lounge, before the game, a director approached her and asked, 'Excuse me, are you reading a book?' 'Yes,' my wife replied, expecting some sort of conversation about the book. But the director was in a state of shock. Clearly, he had never seen a woman read before. He finally muttered, 'Oh,' before walking away. That made Ann's mind up: the place was in the dark ages. I think she half expected the fans to stone us if we made a mistake and for the locals to point at the sun and shout, 'Bright light, bright light.' I kept telling her we weren't in Swansea! On the way home she informed me, in no uncertain terms, 'If you think I'm moving up here you've got another thing coming.'

Despite my Ann's reservations I loved my time at Rochdale. Playing at Spotland was a great experience. The ground wasn't the best, and it was falling apart even then, but it always had a good atmosphere. It was tiny in comparison to Ninian Park, but despite the fact that Rochdale were in a relegation battle in the fourth tier of English football they were still getting crowds bigger than Cardiff. It was sad really, and showed me just how far *my* team had slumped. However, just as had been the case at Cardiff, the Rochdale fans took me into their hearts and made me feel very welcome.

Feeling wanted by a manager, and by the fans, as well as playing at a lower level, saw me play some of my best football in ages. Yes,

Big Joe and I enjoyed the physical side of the game, but with so much time and space I found that even with my ageing legs, and bad knee, I could knock the ball around with ease. My confidence came flooding back and before long I had helped lift Rochdale out of the relegation zone, courtesy of me scoring the winner in a crunch game against our fellow strugglers, Southend.

By the end of the season we were in seventeenth place and avoided dropping out of the league, which would have spelt disaster for the club. I was very proud of the part I had played in their survival. Not only because it showed that I still had something to offer in professional football, but also because Vic Hallom had given me a chance and I felt I had justified his faith. At the end of the season it was great to hear Vic tell the press, 'I thought players like Phil Dwyer were extinct.' I think he meant it as a compliment.

With the season at an end I had a difficult decision to make regarding my future. Rochdale were keen for me to stay another season, and while I had really enjoyed my time there I didn't fancy a year of travelling up and down the motorway every week. Swansea and Newport were also rumoured to be interested, particularly after I had proven my worth. But did I want to play on? I was now thirty-four, my knee wasn't getting any better and I had achieved everything I had ever hoped to achieve in the game. Playing for Cardiff, and then Wales, had surpassed my wildest dreams and I began to think that I had enjoyed a good run and that maybe I should quit now, while I could still walk.

As I pondered my decision a good friend of mine, who worked for the police, asked if I had ever thought of joining the force. The thought had never crossed my mind, but he said that I would be perfect for it, and also that I would enjoy it. The more I thought about it the more I liked the idea.

After discussing the move with Ann we both agreed that now was the perfect time to finish with football and the police would be a good place for me to forge a new career. I loved football, and it was not a decision I took lightly, but in my heart of hearts I knew it was the right decision. For a while I dreamt of a phone call from Cardiff, asking me to come back in some capacity, but it never came. I would have done anything they asked of me and I believe that I could have given the club a lot in return but it wasn't to be. My time as one of the boys in the blue of Cardiff City was over and I was now about to become a boy in blue for the South Wales police.

# 21

## Boy in Blue

Leaving the cocoon of the football world behind was a culture shock and at times I wondered if I had made the right decision. As I sat in a classroom, learning the law, I would think of my mates, who were still playing and wish I was still with them. I don't think it was the playing side that I missed so much, more the dressing-room environment, where you can act like a big kid, no matter your age. Joining the police I felt as though I had to grow up, and be on my best behaviour, but I soon learned that everyone loved a laugh and a joke just as much as me.

I think thirty was the age limit for joining the force, but as I was older I was given special dispensation, which earned me a few choice remarks. Despite this I soon settled in and proved that I had what it took. To my surprise I sailed through my exams and even got 100 per cent in one test. At school I had never paid attention, as my mind was dominated by sport, but I suppose I had now matured, and realised I had a family to provide for, so I knuckled down and proved I wasn't just a pretty face!

Once I had passed the exams I began working at Barry police station, where I would be on the beat for shifts that usually lasted eight hours. At any one time there would be about twenty of us working in a team and it was like being back in the dressing room. The banter, the nicknames, the jokes; they were all there and some were even cruder than the ones I had heard in football. I soon learned that it's vital there is a good team spirit in the police because day in, day out you are involved in some pretty intense situations and need to be able to trust colleagues with your life.

During my two-year probationary period on the beat I had two fantastic tutors in Glynn Jones and Joe Erskine. In stature they were complete opposites. Glynn was so small that I am sure he must have worn stacked heels when the height requirement was being assessed. Joe, on the other hand, had no such trouble as he was six foot five and must have weighed over twenty stones. The mere sight of him put the fear of God into those who were up to no good. Those two helped me no end by showing me the ropes and keeping my nose clean.

I always remember that on my first day at Barry I was eager to get cracking so at the start of my shift I bounded out of the station ready for action. Big Joe, strolling nonchalantly behind me, gave me my first telling off.

'Oi, Phil. Come here.'

Thinking I was already in trouble I turned back.

'What's the matter, Joe?' I asked

'Listen. We've got eight hours of this and I don't need you setting off like Seb Coe,' he replied.

I soon knew what he meant. Walking the beat was hard work, tedious at times, and you had to conserve energy for when it was really needed.

In the late 1980s Barry was divided into sectors and in each sector there would be two officers on the beat at all times. My sector would usually be the top of Holton Road, which stretched for miles, and as a result there would be six officers working on that one road. All day long you would walk down your allocated sector and then up again, keeping an eye out for trouble, and letting people know that you were in the neighbourhood.

Even though I was from a hard, working-class area like Grangetown, and thought I had seen most things, Barry was an eye-opener. As a kid I was a toe rag from time to time but I always respected the police and if I ever saw an officer I would keep my mouth shut and cross the road out of respect. But some of the kids I encountered didn't know the meaning of the word respect. They loved nothing more than to shower you with insults as soon as they saw you. Because it happened so often you couldn't arrest everyone who spoke to you in that manner, so in the end you had to laugh, or ignore it, and keep your eyes peeled for more serious crimes.

It was hard at times, but I didn't have it as bad as some of my fellow officers thanks to my status as a former Cardiff City player. Plenty of people would recognise me and say hello, even those that I knew full well were shady characters. Having played for Cardiff was a big plus as people thought they knew me, and as a result it made some respect me, whereas in normal circumstances they would be bombarding the police with abuse. In the end I got to know a number of the villains quite well. They were polite to me and I was polite back but we both knew that if I caught them at it I wouldn't have any hesitation about taking them down.

Catching those who were up to no good gave me a real kick and the adrenalin rush was similar to scoring a goal. One of my first collars occurred when I was on the beat one night with a fellow officer called Daryl, whom I nicknamed 'Jack', due to the fact that he was from Swansea. As we were walking the back lanes of Holton Road we heard a commotion coming from a nearby shop. Just as we started to run towards the back entrance two guys came running towards us, laden with goods they had just stolen. Talk about getting caught red-handed.

It turned out to be the easiest collar of my career but Daryl and I both got a pat on the back for being there, even if we hadn't had to do much. I think that arrest clearly shows the benefit of having police constantly on the beat. These days I know for a fact that there is nowhere near the level of police out and about as there was in my time. I think it is a shame because crooks keep their heads down if they know police are walking the streets, but these days they can do what they like. By the time a police car has turned up, they have scarpered, and it is very difficult to catch them. A lot of my friends who still work for the police tell me that nowadays they spend more time doing admin than catching crooks. Some of them are bored stiff and can't wait to retire.

The criminals in Barry really had to work for it in the late 1980s. They certainly weren't stupid and used a number of ruses to divert our attention. One of their favourite ploys was to cause a ruckus at one end of Barry, which would see most of us head down there to help out. While we were occupied they would be up to no good at the other end of the town. Soon we became wise to their tricks and they had to work even harder to get us off our regular beat.

I had always considered myself to be quite polite, but I soon learned that in some cases good manners don't pay off. If you tried to reason with some criminals they didn't respect you and would try to walk all over you. Asking some of the blokes I caught, 'Excuse me sir, do you mind accompanying me to the police station?' wouldn't get me very far. Sadly, you had to be quite abrasive and to show them that you weren't going to be messed around. You had to grab hold of them hard, and perhaps even shout and swear, in order to get their attention. It was just like being captain of Cardiff City!

Police wouldn't get away with it today as they would be the ones who would end up in the dock, but to me that is political correctness gone mad. By no means am I advocating shouting, swearing and being hard in all situations; in certain cases, however, it is necessary, because it is the only thing that some people understand. A laugh and a joke will often suffice to neutralise a situation, but even that is frowned upon. The powers that be need to trust officers to analyse a situation and to deploy the tactics they think will work best. I know it is a source of real frustration for some officers that they have to behave like robots.

Back then you also had a fair amount of discretion when it came to arresting people involved in a crime. For instance, I remember one night Daryl and I were walking near a park when we heard a groaning noise in the bushes. We went to investigate and as we got closer we realised it was a guy and a girl, completely starkers, having it off. It was an embarrassing situation so I tried to make a noise by scuffing my shoes on the ground to let them know we were around but they kept going. In the end I had to flash my torch in their faces, which had them jumping up in shock, and legging it with their pants around their ankles.

Yes, they were breaking the law, but it was the middle of the night, it was pitch black and no one was around. What harm were they doing? Besides, the fact that we stumbled upon them caused them so much embarrassment that they would certainly think twice before engaging in that sort of behaviour again. No doubt they would be arrested these days, which could lead to great embarrassment, and even the loss of their jobs. Is that sort of offence worth such a harsh punishment when it is done in the middle of the night, with no one around? I don't think so.

Working for the police was an absolute pleasure. I loved every minute. I really felt I was making a difference and that I was helping to keep the streets safe. Sometimes I would catch criminals, sometimes I wouldn't, but I certainly made sure they couldn't sleep easily and by and large I did my job well. Often it was a thankless task but it was a task that had to be done and the thrill of catching someone in the act was tremendous. Unfortunately, all good things have to come to an end, and my time in the police ended on a distinctly sour note.

In 2000 I was working on a murder case in Bridgend. One day a colleague of mine picked me up from home as we had to go across to Weston-super-Mare to interview a witness. It had been arranged that once we were done we would meet our workmates in Bridgend for a few drinks before catching the train to Cardiff to hit a few bars. As planned, once we had finished in Weston, we made our way to Bridgend, but an incident had occurred so a number of the boys were delayed. Consequently, we decided to wait in the pub for them and not bother going into Cardiff.

At throwing-out time I went to get some chips before realising that the last train to Cardiff had come and gone. I didn't have my car with me so I tried to ring a few taxis but was told there would be a long wait. Sometimes a fellow officer, who was working in Bridgend, would be called down to Cardiff so I rang around to see if anyone could give me a lift on their way but no joy. Stranded in Bridgend, and slightly inebriated, I made one of the stupidest decisions of my life.

In my pocket I had the keys to one of the unmarked police cars at the station. Foolishly, I thought I was sober enough to drive the car home and that I could return it the next day. I reasoned that my last drink had been over an hour ago and that the good meal I had eaten would have soaked up some of the alcohol in my system.

Without a second thought I set off for Cardiff in the unmarked car, and although I thought I was sober, I hadn't counted on how tired

I was. At some point I fell asleep behind the wheel and proceeded to wrap the car around a lamppost. Incredibly, there were no other cars on the road at the time so no one else was involved. Shortly after the crash, as I sat dazed, and in pain, behind the wheel, the paramedics and the police turned up.

When the police got to me I was struggling to breathe, due to damaged ribs, so they were unable to breathalyse me. When I got to hospital they took a blood sample and it turned out that I was well over the limit. I couldn't believe how stupid I had been. Not only had I risked my life and career but also I was incredibly lucky that I hadn't hurt anyone. If I had, I don't know if I would have been able to live with myself.

Recovering from broken ribs I was laid up in hospital for four weeks. The pain was unbearable at times. Every time I breathed, sneezed or moved I flinched, but I suppose it was the least I deserved. While I was in hospital the story of my misdemeanour made the local news and this caused acute embarrassment to me and more importantly to my wife and family. Ann was mortified, and I can't tell you how sorry I was to see her so upset. I had let her, my kids, myself and my fellow officers down. Why hadn't I waited for a taxi or grabbed a hotel room in Bridgend? It is a question that haunts me to this day.

When I was released from hospital I went to court where I faced charges of the aggravated taking of a police vehicle and drink driving. Both were serious crimes, especially for a member of the force, and I knew I was fighting for my career. I held my hands up and pleaded guilty, prepared to take any punishment that came my way, which turned out to be a stiff fine and a twelve-month driving ban. Eventually it became clear that if I tried to stay on with the police I would be sacked, so I jumped before I was pushed and handed in my resignation.

Leaving the police in such a manner hurt me immensely and to be honest I really struggled for a time. I had ruined fifteen years of good service thanks to a moment of madness. There was, however, no time to feel sorry for myself as I needed to get back to work, in some capacity, as quickly as possible. Thankfully, I didn't have to wait too long for an opportunity to present itself.

During my time in the police I got to know plenty of solicitors. One of them was Steve Clarke, a partner at the firm, Clarke and Hartland. Steve had heard about my troubles and said that, if I was interested, his firm had a vacancy for someone to deal with Crown Court work. In my position it was a no-brainer. I jumped at the chance.

I had gone full circle and it was a strange feeling. An important part of my job was to attend police stations and advise people of their rights under questioning. Countless times I was the police officer on the other side of the table, and I like to think that I know every trick in the book. It is vital that those who are arrested get proper representation, and aren't treated as criminals before a court has made its judgement, as I have lost count of the amount of times someone who was fingered for a crime turned out to be innocent.

When you first attend a client in a cell they are usually stressed and scared. It is important to calm them down, let them know their rights and explain what the process ahead entails. It is a big responsibility, but one that is vital to the proper administration of justice. Some are so scared they will say anything so it is vital that you make them feel secure and impress on them that they just have to tell the truth, no matter what pressure comes their way.

My time working on both sides of the table has led to some amusing incidents. I was once called to Barry police station to meet with a client in order to discuss his case before questioning started. When I walked into the interview room I introduced myself and started talking but my client just stared at me blankly and bluntly said, 'If you're going to interview me shouldn't you put the tapes on first.' I explained to him that I was there to discuss his case and there was no need for tapes, but he replied, 'I know you. You're a policeman, you work here. What do you think you're playing at?' It turned out I had arrested him during my time in the force and that he remembered me. After briefly explaining my career change we had a good laugh about it, but I've had that happen to me a few times now.

Sometimes I'll be in a room with a client and they will say, 'I know you.' Usually I'll think that I must have dealt with them before, from my days in the police, so I'll explain that I now work for a firm of solicitors. But more often than not they will say, 'No, that's not it.' Then I'll twig, they are Cardiff fans and recognise me from the football. When I tell them my name they want to spend more time discussing Cardiff City than their case!

I've been very fortunate with my career since I left football. When I realised that my time in the game was coming to an end I didn't have a clue what I was going to do with myself and was terrified of the future. I count myself lucky that in the police I found a profession that I enjoyed and that a twist of fate has led me into another career that really motivates me.

Since leaving professional football I have continued to play the game. There was no way I could leave it completely. Over the years I have continued to play for, and coach, semi-professional teams such as Cardiff Civil Service, Grange Quinns and Cardiff Corries. I also represented the South Wales police team, when they reached the first division of the Welsh League, and it was also great fun to be called up for the Welsh police team for games against our English, Irish and Scottish counterparts.

Sadly, my knee continued to give me bother so I had to cut down on my playing when I reached my mid-forties, although I still had the occasional game, even agreeing to play in goal. To this day I find it hard to turn down a game and I can't resist turning out for the ex Cardiff City team in charity games. More than the playing I really enjoy the camaraderie of the dressing room. It always cheers me up seeing old faces and having the same banter that we had over thirty years ago. I don't think I will ever tire of it.

Leaving Ninian Park was a huge wrench and for a while the state of the club really upset me. After I left, City gradually went downhill and spent years yo-yoing between the old third and fourth divisions. I would still go to games as a fan, if I wasn't playing myself, and it seemed that the club was in terminal decline. We didn't look to be going anywhere and at times the club was hanging on for dear life just to remain in existence.

Of course, since Sam Hammam arrived in 1999 the club has changed beyond all recognition. There have been hiccups along the way but no City fan can complain at where we are right now. As I write we are in a brand-new stadium, have a state-of-the-art training facility down the Vale and a squad littered with internationals. With a bright young manager like Malky Mackay I am sure we will do well in the 2011/12 Championship. When you consider where we have been it is quite incredible.

Never in a million years did I think that in my lifetime I would see Cardiff City play at Wembley, let alone three times in the space of two years. We may not have won the FA Cup, or the Championship play-off final in 2010, but the club is heading in the right direction. It was incredible to see Wembley rammed with over forty thousand Cardiff fans, and then the new stadium getting crowds regularly topping twenty thousand. In my day we would sometimes get crowds of just three thousand, even when we were playing in the equivalent of the Championship.

It was of course sad that the club had to leave Ninian Park. I had so many great times there and I considered it a second home. However, for the club to progress, and to bring in more revenue, it needed a modern, all-seater stadium, with hospitality boxes, club shop and top-class catering facilities. I do like the new stadium but Ninian Park will always have a place in my heart. Sometimes I shut my eyes and think of the old Grange End stretching all the way back, crammed with fanatical supporters, swaying like a wave, chanting and cheering, with the smell of fried onions and tobacco wafting down onto the pitch and the ferocious roar when someone in a blue shirt scored. It was magical. Those days are sadly gone but I count myself lucky that I got to experience them. No doubt, in time, the new stadium will have its own unique character and atmosphere and we will grow to love it just as we did Ninian Park.

Finally, the sleeping giant appears to have awoken and there is a real buzz about the place. These days, in the city, you see just as many kids wearing Cardiff shirts as those of Manchester United. If Cardiff could have a prolonged period in the Premier League, with a little bit of success, I am convinced we could get crowds of over forty thousand on a regular basis. The club has a huge catchment area, with thousands of fans coming from the Valleys, as well as from Cardiff itself. I am also convinced that plenty of football fans would also come down from other parts of Wales, and the south-west, if we had Premiership football here.

I still go to watch Cardiff to this day, usually with my son-in-law, but I can't claim to be a good-luck charm. I think at one point I didn't see them win for nine months and everyone who I sat by begged me to stop going. Thankfully, I finally broke the curse when Ross McCormack struck two late goals against Burnley a few years back.

Cardiff fans continue to amaze me to this day. Their loyalty is second to none. They are mad supporters and if you give them 100 per cent they will give it back to you tenfold. Some fans are absolutely nuts and I honestly couldn't tell you some of the crazy requests I've had down the years. Probably the funniest one came after the last ever game at Ninian Park, which was against Ipswich Town. I was having a drink in the Ninian Park pub when a bloke came up to me with a huge blue toilet door under his arm and asked me to sign it. It turned out that he had taken it from the stadium as a souvenir. God knows what he was going to do with it.

I have been blessed to have enjoyed such a great career and to have such a fantastic family. Ann and I are still happily married while our children, Darren and Claire, continue to be our pride and joy, even though they are now all grown up and Claire has children of her own. It is a real thrill to be a granddad to little Luca and Erin and I've already got them in training with a football, in the hope that one day they may follow their granddad Phil and become a Bluebird.

Looking back on my career I don't have many regrets. By and large I achieved all of my goals and got to live out my dreams. However, one thing that has always intrigued me is what sort of reception would I have received at Ninian Park if I had run out in a Swansea shirt? Would the fans remember the good times and cheer me or would I have become a pantomime villain? I'll never find out the answer to that one.

I've had a marvellous time, full of ups and downs, laughter and tears and I couldn't have wished for anything more. To be born in Cardiff, and to have the opportunity to walk out at Ninian Park, in that famous blue shirt, in front of a full house chanting my name, is an experience I will always cherish. I have to thank you, the fans, for all the support you have given me over the years, and continue to give me. You've all been great.

It's been lovely reminiscing about the past, discussing incidents, players and games I haven't thought about in a long time and I hope you've enjoyed reading my recollections just as much as I've enjoyed telling them. Whatever happens in the future at Cardiff we know it will be a rollercoaster, but just think, after all of the lows we've had to endure, how we will enjoy the highs when they come, which inevitably they will. One thing is for sure, I'll be partying with the rest of you.

Here's to a successful Cardiff City team in the Premier League!

# 22

# Dream Team

Over the years I have been asked this question countless times: 'Who would make up your perfect Cardiff City squad from your time at the club?' To be honest my answer changes every time I am asked, as I played with so many good players, but after a few discussions in the pub this is the team I've come up with.

### Goalkeeper: Ron Healey

I suppose it has to be a toss-up between Ron Healey and Bill Irwin. Ron was Joe Corrigan's understudy at Manchester City and had a great pedigree while Bill came through Irish football to sign for Cardiff, where he proceeded to win the BBC 'Save of the Season' award after an outstanding block against Leeds United in 1972.

Both were great leaders on the pitch, commanding their penalty area, speaking to their defenders and making brave saves. I always felt confident playing in front of them because they would be constantly speaking to me, helping me with my positioning and making me aware of what the opposition were doing out of my line of sight.

It is a tough one but I would probably opt for Ron because he was a slightly better shot stopper and was more consistent. You need to have confidence in your keeper and with Ron you knew that nine times out of ten he would be flawless. If a ball came into the box he would batter everyone out of the way to make it his. I used to step aside when he came for the ball, to avoid getting whacked, and more often than not he would catch it cleanly. Such was Ron's form in goal, during his time at Cardiff, that he was also capped by the Republic of Ireland.

### Right Back: Linden Jones

I always liked Linden Jones at right back. He was a solid, hard-tackling full back, who always put in a shift, and he could play a bit as well. Linden was from the Valleys, hard as nails, and not many would get past him, as he was quick as well. In 1979 he earned the distinction of being the youngest player to have ever got sent off for Cardiff City but he was a rock in the promotion-winning team of 1982/83. With Linden at full back I could rest easy that no winger would get an easy ride.

### Centre Back: Don Murray

We had some outstanding centre backs during my time at the club, men such as Mike England, Don Murray, Brian Harris, Leighton Phillips and Gary Bennett. This is a tough one to call as they were all exceptional in one area and if you could mould all of these players together you would come close to the perfect defender.

As I played alongside him for so long, and he was an inspiration to me, I would go for Don Murray for one of the positions. He was a fantastic leader, who really put his body on the line for the club, and the fans loved him. Making over four hundred appearances for the club he was also a key figure in the club's push for promotion in 1971 and more than held his own in the thrilling European clashes with Hamburg and Real Madrid.

### Centre Back: Yours Truly

In order to save any arguments, and because it is my team, I am going to pick myself as the second centre back. I am also going to make myself captain. No doubt a few of the boys will be having words with me next time I see them, but I can't please everyone. Besides, I wouldn't want to miss the opportunity to play alongside Don again, although we might be struggling for pace these days, but then again, we always were!

## Left Back: Gary Bell

Gary Bell was excellent in this position and was an important part of the team that almost got promoted to the first division under Jimmy Scoular. Clive Charles, John Lewis and Paul Bodin also did very well there, but I have to go for Belly as he'll be reading this and I don't think I can put up with his sulking if he's not in the team. Besides I may even get a pint out of it!

In all honesty Belly was a class act, despite giving away two penalties on his debut in a 7–1 loss to Wolves in 1966. To be fair he had a fantastic left peg and could knock the ball all over the field with amazing accuracy. It was also very rare that you saw a winger get past him and for these reasons he more than earns his place.

## Right Midfield: Willie Anderson

The two names that spring instantly to mind in this position are Dave Bennett and Willie Anderson. Willie was a superb player, who had great experience from his days at Manchester United and Aston Villa. If you gave him the ball you knew he would keep it. He also had quick feet and possibly the best delivery I saw in my time in the second division. During the 1975/76 promotion-winning season he set up so many goals for Adrian Alston and Tony Evans it was unreal.

Benno was a different type of winger. He relied very much on his explosive pace and tricks to beat a man but he could also whip in a good cross and had an eye for goal. I know Jeff Hemmerman loved playing with him as he was a great source of supply for our forwards. When he left us, to join Coventry City in the first division, he continued his success by winning the FA Cup in 1987.

I may surprise a few people here but I think I would go for Willie to start, but it's a close one. Benno would have to be on the bench, pushing him hard for his place.

## Central Midfield: Alan Campbell

Again, this was a position where we were blessed with some real talent and it makes it enormously difficult to pick just two. We had the likes of Alan Campbell, Doug Livermore, Nigel Vaughan, Roger Gibbins and John Buchanan during my time at Cardiff and they were all tremendously gifted players.

Alan Campbell was always a favourite of mine so I suppose I would have to pick him for one of the spots. Before joining us he had enjoyed a good career at both Charlton and Birmingham, where he earned a reputation for being one of the best passers of the ball outside of the top flight. At Cardiff he was a pleasure to play with and some of his passes took my breath away.

## Central Midfield: John Buchanan

In the other centre midfield spot I have to pick John Buchanan. His thunderous strike against Swansea more than justifies his inclusion, but he was someone you always wanted in your team. Buchy could not only put his foot in, but he also got more than his fair share of goals from the centre of the park. In fact he finished as the club's top scorer in two out of the seven seasons he was with us.

When Alan signed for us in the promotion season of 1975/76 he and Buchy were tremendous together in the middle and made a formidable duo. Reunited, in my team, they would really protect Don and me and create and score plenty of goals as well.

## Left Midfield: John Lewis

John Lewis was spotted playing local football, and although he was initially just a part-time player with us, he soon became a permanent fixture in the first team. John could play at the back, as well as in midfield, and I don't think he ever let us down. He was so fit he would get up and down that wing all day long, helping out in defence, before surging forward and getting involved in the attack. I think that Belly and him would really work well together on the left flank and as they both had great left feet we would have a tremendous supply line from this side of the field.

**Centre Forwards: Adrian Alston and Tony Evans**

I was privileged to play with some fabulous attacking talent, guys like Bob Hatton, Robin Friday, Brian Clark, Peter Kitchen and Jeff Hemmerman but I don't think you could find a better partnership than Adrian Alston and Tony Evans. In the season they played together in the old third division they were untouchable and scored all sorts of goals. Defenders didn't have a clue what they were going to do, but the two of them just clicked.

Tony and Adrian would be a match for most defenders when they were on song and I would love to see them lead the line together again. When they both eventually departed – Adrian to the USA and Evo to Birminghan – they did well, but they were never the same without each other. Their understanding was telepathic at times.

**Substitutes**

Thankfully, you are allowed to name seven subs in the modern game, so my bench would be as follows:

Bill Irwin
Jeff Hemmerman
Robin Friday
Mike England
Leighton Phillips
Gary Bennett
Dave Bennett

**Manager**

During my time at Cardiff City one manager towered over all others: Jimmy Scoular. Perhaps I am a little biased, because he gave me my chance in the game, but I think most of the players who played for him would agree that he was a great manager. He had an incredible aura and love him or loathe him he made you want to run through brick walls. Everyone respected him, and I think he managed to get an extra 10 per cent out of players, simply because no one wanted to let him down. He didn't have much money to spend, but he built a team with a mixture of graft and flair that not only came close to being promoted to the first division but also reached the semi-final of the European Cup Winners Cup. Jimmy loved the game, and he loved Cardiff City Football Club, and I think if anyone could get my team playing to its full potential it would be him.

I'm sure many will disagree with my choices but that's the beauty of football, so much of it is subjective. Hopefully, it will give you something to talk about over a pint in the pub and it will allow you to reminisce about some of the greatest players to have worn the blue shirt of Cardiff City . . . and Gary Bell!